An Invitation to

Safety Conversations

An Invitation to

Safety Conversations

REAL DIALOGUE
BETTER WORK

DANIEL HUMMERDAL

ISBN 978-1-7645701-0-7 (paperback)
ISBN 978-1-7645701-1-4 (hardback)
ISBN 978-1-7645701-2-1 (ebook)

First published 2026
Published by Open Change Press
Brisbane, Australia

Cover and interior design by Karolina Kruk-Umięcka
Edited by Claire McGregor

Table of contents

Foreword

By Tony Hetherington
Former Head of Energy Division, Health and Safety Executive (GB)
Former Head of High Hazards, Energy and Public Safety, WorkSafe New Zealand

Anyone responsible for safety will recognise the problem. The hardware is in place. The training has been delivered. The procedures are written. And yet accidents still happen, and work doesn't follow plans. There is a persistent gap between expected and actual performance. This book sets out a thoughtful yet practical way of using conversation to explore why that gap exists. But what matters here is not technique alone, but how those conversations are approached, and the stance taken toward the people involved.

Reading this book caused me to reflect on my own career: over thirty years as a regulator with Great Britain's Health and Safety Executive, followed by three years with WorkSafe New Zealand. Data, metrics, and formal evidence were always an important part of inspection work. But the real insights so often came from understanding how work was actually done. And that understanding came from conversation.

As a frontline inspector, I learned quickly that opening an inspection with direct questions about safety performance rarely helped to establish meaningful dialogue. It was far more productive to start by building rapport and trying to understand how the people in front of me saw their roles, their responsibilities, and the pressures they were working under. Appreciating those pressures was essential if I was to understand why work as imagined by senior leaders often differed so markedly from work as actually done.

Despite this, I frequently observed safety advisers and managers relying almost exclusively on simplistic performance metrics to understand safety. Lost-time injury rates, slips and trips, and other easily measured indicators were often presented as evidence that risks were well controlled. Meanwhile, deeper issues such as asset integrity or the control of major fire and explosion hazards received far less attention. I always felt that both safety professionals and business leaders lacked effective ways to peel back layers of misunderstanding. They lacked the tools to shine light on misconceptions about how their businesses really functioned. This book provides those tools.

Too often, safety performance is judged by what is easiest to count rather than what most needs to be understood. I have repeatedly been assured by senior industry figures that their risks are under control, only to find that the people with the deepest understanding of the operation, the people at the sharp end, had concerns that were not travelling upward. This disconnect creates complacency and runs counter to Dame Judith Hackitt's advice that those responsible for managing major hazards should always retain a sense of unease about how well risks are being controlled.

When differences in safety performance between sites were identified, the response was frequently predictable: bring the poorer performers up to standard by increasing controls, supervision, or oversight. Far less attention was paid to understanding why some sites performed better than others. Why not ask what enables good performance? What attributes, conditions, and practices support it? And how might those be strengthened and sustained? This book explores those questions. It argues that focusing solely on eliminating failure is insufficient, and that understanding why work goes well is essential to achieving lasting improvement.

In the major hazard sector, we also talk frequently about the importance of detecting weak signals: early indications that systems, plant, or processes are not functioning as intended, or that standards are beginning to erode. Too often, these signals remain weak because they are dampened by distance, hierarchy, or poor communication between the frontline and those with the authority to act. Better conversations can reduce this attenuation. There is no clearer illustration of this than the Deepwater Horizon disaster. In the period leading up to the explosion, senior leaders visited the installation. They were talking to staff and reviewing safety. But they failed to engage in the right conversations; ones that might have revealed the developing risks in time to intervene.

The approach set out in this book helps address that problem. Throughout my career, I tried to have better conversations. Here, Daniel Hummerdal has carefully examined that practice and provided a systematic way of doing it well. I wish this level of thinking, analysis, and practical guidance had been available to me earlier in my career.

It is important to be clear about what this book is not saying. Conversation is not a substitute for basic safety measures. Sound engineering controls, safe access, guarding, ventilation, and competent supervision must already be in place. But for organisations that have invested in these fundamentals, better conversations can add significant value. They can reveal whether those controls are functioning as intended and whether they are being supported, or undermined, by everyday work practices.

These conversations are not easy. They require planning, patience, and skill. They demand that we resist the temptation to provide answers too quickly and that we remain open to having our assumptions challenged. Someone capable of conducting these conversations well is a genuine asset to any organisation. And importantly, conversation carries an obligation: when people share their insights, action must follow. Understanding without response quickly erodes trust.

Although this book focuses on safety, its relevance extends further. As I read the developing drafts, I became increasingly convinced that these techniques apply equally to other areas of regulation and management, including environmental protection, waste management, and broader operational performance. Managers with wider responsibilities may find that applying these approaches in other domains yields insights they did not expect.

One of the most important reminders in this book is that, in these conversations, we are not the experts. The people doing the work hold the knowledge. If we already had the answers, there would be no need for the conversation in the first place. We must be prepared to listen, to learn, and to accept that what we hear may challenge our beliefs. And we must be prepared to act on what we learn, even when that action is uncomfortable.

Understanding how work is actually done is essential if we are to improve safety. This book offers a practical way to do that. By using the conversational approaches described here, organisations can move toward genuinely engaging their workforce as part of the solution, rather than continuing to treat them as the problem.

Better conversations help us understand why things usually go right, how good performance is sustained, and what conditions make failure more likely. Acting on that understanding improves safety, protects workers and the public, and helps ensure that investment in safety delivers real value. In my view, this book makes a serious and timely contribution to that effort.

Preface

The distance between "How do I get you to do X?" and "How do we improve X?" seems small – just a shift in pronouns, a minor grammatical adjustment. But it's a shift that changes how we organise work.

The first question assumes separation. It positions you as the one with answers and them as the ones who need to comply. It maintains the us/them divide that most organisations struggle with, but few know how to close.

The second question invites partnership. It acknowledges that neither of you has the complete picture alone. It requires both sides to step into the same space, make sense of the same reality, and work together towards something better.

This book is about how to make that shift, not just in your words, but in how you show up, listen, and create space for truth to travel. It's about conversations that close distance rather than manage it, that build "we" where there has been separation.

The transformation begins with a willingness to ask different questions, to listen differently, and enter the conversation as a partner rather than a problem-solver or enforcer.

Why conversation matters

Over fifteen years of working with mining, construction, utilities, and aviation organisations, I've watched the same pattern repeat: organisations implement safety programs that don't change behaviour, conduct investigations that blame individuals for system failures, and create metrics to track performance, but go blind to what matters. Meanwhile, the people closest to the work, the ones with the clearest view of what's happening, remain largely unheard.

When organisations do acknowledge the need for a more open-ended "let's talk about it" approach, they often proceduralise the practice. They create conversation programs, develop question banks, and train leaders in techniques. What gets missed is an appreciation for what real conversation requires: the inner qualities, the relational ground, the willingness to be changed by what you hear.

This book is an invitation into that space. It doesn't offer scripts or a formula to follow. Instead, it offers language, ways of seeing, and practices that help you create conversations where people feel able to speak honestly about what makes work difficult or dangerous, and what makes it possible or better. It is about conversations that bring intelligence and collaboration back into the system.

The central challenge

Every organisation faces a fundamental tension: as they grow and scale, distance increases between those who design work and those who do it. Leaders move further from the frontline. Functions separate into silos and hierarchy creates layers. What might have once been a shared "we" fragments into "us" and "them", managers and workers, designers and recipients, those who decide and those who experience the consequences of those decisions.

Most organisations accept this fragmentation as inevitable. They manage it through systems, such as cascading communication, escalation processes, performance metrics, and compliance verification. The logic is simple: since we can't all know each other, we'll coordinate through structure and control.

But something essential gets lost in translation. The lived experience of work, the pressures people navigate, the trade-offs they make, the intelligence they bring to impossible situations, doesn't travel well through formal channels. It gets filtered, smoothed, and abstracted until what reaches decision-makers bears little resemblance to reality.

Weak signals die in the gap between levels, workarounds remain hidden, and adaptations that keep work functioning go unrecognised. The distance widens, and with it, the organisation's ability to understand itself diminishes.

This book argues for a different approach, where conversation is the primary mechanism through which organisations stay in contact with themselves.

And not conversation as another program to implement or metric to track either, but as a relational practice that closes the distance control systems create. Conversation should help both sides see what the other sees and make constraints discussable rather than hidden. It should allow solutions to emerge from joint sensemaking rather than being imposed from above.

When this happens – when conversation becomes real – the us/them fracture begins to heal and partnership becomes possible, while safety stops being something done to people and becomes something built with them.

Who this book is for

This book is for anyone whose conversations shape how work happens.

Safety professionals will likely recognise themselves first. You know the limits of traditional tools. You feel the frustration of knowing that real safety lives somewhere beyond checklists, audits, and campaigns. This book offers language and practices to help you work more relationally, more intelligently, and closer to how work happens.

But you don't need "safety" in your title for this book to matter. Supervisors, managers, team leads, and project managers are having the conversations that count every day.

Inspectors and regulators occupy a difficult position. You assess and assure safety from outside the system. You see the gap between what can be inspected and what truly matters. Conversations sit at that boundary; they shape what people choose to reveal, what stays hidden, and how systems respond to what they hear. This book offers ways to deepen understanding without weakening accountability.

Auditors may find this book unsettling ... and helpful. Auditing focuses on what can be verified, while conversations reveal what can't. Many risks and possibilities live in that gap. If your work involves asking questions, interpreting evidence, and making judgements about system health, this book invites you to listen differently to what people are telling you, and what they're not.

Consultants and advisors who work across organisations will recognise the patterns in these pages. You've seen what happens when conversation breaks down and what becomes possible when it returns. This book gives you the language and structure for the work you may already be doing intuitively.

Executives and senior leaders shape the conditions in which all other conversations happen. You may not spend much time on the floor anymore, but the quality of conversation throughout your organisation depends on what you model, protect, and reward. Chapter 11 explores conversational leadership in depth, but the entire book is relevant to how you create the relational ground on which performance rests.

Although titled *An Invitation to Safety Conversations*, the practices here apply wherever performance depends on judgement, coordination, learning, and care, which is nearly everywhere work matters. The examples come from safety, but the same conversational approach matters in quality, operations, maintenance, reliability, human resources, and change work of all kinds. Wherever people are trying to make work work better under real conditions, conversation is doing more of the heavy lifting than most systems recognise.

You don't need to agree with everything here to find value in it. You don't need to abandon standards, rules, or oversight. What this book invites is a shift in perspective, from extracting answers to making sense together, from checking to listening, from performing safety to practising it.

If you spend time talking with people about work, risk, responsibility, or improvement, this book is an invitation to make those conversations more honest, more human, and more useful.

This book is structured into three parts.

Part One: Foundations (Chapters 1–3) makes the case for why conversation matters and what it requires. Chapter 1 shows what becomes possible when organisations shift from control to partnership. Chapter 2 examines why organisations lose contact with themselves and how conversation can restore it. Chapter

3 explores the inner qualities that make real conversation possible – curiosity, compassion, and courage.

Part Two: The Six Conversation Types (Chapters 4–9) offers practical frameworks for different conversational purposes. Connection creates the relational ground. Learning reveals how work happens. Appreciative conversations bring to the surface what enables success. Possibility conversations help imagination take shape. Accountability conversations connect expectations to meaning. Restorative conversations repair what's been strained or broken.

Part Three: From Moments to Movements (Chapters 10–12) shows how conversational practice scales. Chapter 10 explores how individual conversations become organisational capacity. Chapter 11 examines what conversational leadership looks like in practice. Chapter 12 traces the developmental journey from awareness to mastery.

You can read straight through, letting ideas build naturally, or you can jump to what you need now. Sceptical about whether conversation really matters? Start with Chapters 1–3. Want practical guidance immediately? Go to Chapters 4–9. Trying to shift how your whole organisation talks? Head to Chapters 10–12.

You may find that some chapters feel immediately familiar, while others feel less comfortable. This work is developmental, not linear. Take what you need and linger where something resonates. Test what feels useful and return as your context shifts.

If this book opens even one conversation that wouldn't have happened otherwise, it will have done its job.

Daniel Hummerdal
Brisbane, Australia
February 2026

PART ONE

Foundations

CHAPTER 1
An Invitation to Safety Conversations

"What are we like to work for?"

The question hung in the air. For years, Transpower had been asking the tower painters to try harder – be safer, meet targets, comply. Now, for the first time, someone was asking a different question, not demanding or correcting, just ... asking.

The painters shifted in their seats. This wasn't how these conversations usually went.

What came next would transform not just a struggling program, but the entire relationship between the people doing the work and the people managing it. The real breakthrough wasn't in what the painters said, but in the fact that someone had finally *asked.*

The painters' job sounded simple enough: just paint the steel towers so they wouldn't rust. But by 2014 the tower-painting program had become a slow-moving disaster. Costs had blown out, it was behind schedule, quality targets weren't met, and people kept getting hurt.

The response was textbook: technical fixes and tighter control. Engineers redesigned trucks, and managers tightened expectations. There were more rules, more oversight, more accountability. Each intervention got the hopes up that performance would improve, and each time, nothing changed.

> The real breakthrough wasn't in what the painters said, but in the fact that someone had finally asked.

After years of this, the frustration was palpable. Leaders felt they'd done everything "right", and the contractors were cynical. In fact, everyone blamed someone else. The very controls that once gave Transpower confidence were now strangling the work.

Eventually, though, someone did what no one had done in years – they asked the painters, not to try harder, but to talk. The questions were simple, and honest: What's really getting in the way? What are we like to work for? What would make this work safer and better? What ideas do you have that haven't been tried?

The answers that emerged were raw and practical. The painters spoke about short-term contracts that made it impossible to plan ahead. They described tools that didn't work, safety equipment that weighed so much it made work dangerous, trucks with features that weren't needed, and crews that couldn't stay together or be invested in because the work was too uncertain. For years, they had been the recipients of solutions and instructions. At least now their voices were being heard.

Their stories revealed a system working against itself. As the leaders listened, the question changed from "How do we make them comply?" to "How do we make this work actually work?"

Collaboratively, they worked out a suite of changes. First, contracts were extended, giving crews stability. The painters were encouraged to experiment and innovate. New techniques were designed as well as smarter ways to organise the work, and the painters received better vehicles. Personal protective equipment (PPE) weight dropped from twenty kilograms to seven. The relationship shifted from command-and-control to partnership. The painters began approaching Transpower with ideas rather than waiting to be told.

The results stunned everyone. For the first time, the program was delivered in full – productivity had surged. Contractors became profitable and retained skilled people. Transpower made more money too, and the safety incident rate fell from sixty to zero.

What had once been a struggling, low-status program turned into one of the most innovative and successful parts of the business. As Transpower's CEO, Alison Andrew, later reflected, "Safety is so often an outcome. If you have a safety problem, don't just pick away on the safety issue, but look behind to see if there's another reason as to why the business isn't safe."

Stepping into partnership

For years, Transpower had been asking some version of "How can I get you to do X?" Now they were asking something different; something that required partnership.

Most organisations want safety to be a shared responsibility; however, many if not most end up specifying what needs to happen, through supplying designs, observing, counting, detecting, correcting, incentivising, and disciplining. This is what Transpower did, and what most organisations do. But this divides what could be a shared pursuit. It splits the organisation into designers and recipients, into managers and workers, or society into regulators and the regulated, the ones with resources decide what goes, and those that live with the experience of those decisions. This is where Transpower ended up: without a shared understanding of the current state, and without a shared future state that worked for everyone.

However, Transpower found a better framing for their conversation: "How can we improve tower painting?" That question can't be explored from an office, and it can't be answered by the painters alone either. It requires both parties, being in the same place, making sense of the same reality, willing to be honest about what's broken and what could be better.

Realising there was no "we" to begin with, Transpower had to start with the relationship itself. The questions they asked – whether phrased as "What are we like to work for?" or "What's making this difficult for you?" – put the contractors' experience at the centre. These weren't questions about compliance or performance metrics. They were questions about partnership: What's working? What isn't? What do you actually need? There is no telling or fixing in questions like these, just showing up with curiosity to find out what the tower painters knew, with courage to hear potentially uncomfortable truths, and holding the conversation with compassion, not judgement.

The tower painters welcomed that. With an emergent "we" forming, the things that were holding performance back finally found a place to land for tower painters and Transpower.

The pursuit of safety is relational work, not just technical, and it starts with the willingness to enter a conversation as a partner, not a detect-and-correct agent.

Conversations are the "talking cure" for organisations. Just as therapy creates space for what has been avoided to finally be named and integrated, conversation allows organisations to acknowledge what they've been unable to see, speak what has been unspeakable, and work with realities they've been working around. Your organisation holds insight and potential, distributed across the people doing the work. The question is whether the relational ground is strong enough to let those truths surface, be heard, and shape what happens next.

The Transpower transformation wasn't about better procedures or equipment. It was about a different way of working together; one that required the relationship to change first.

The Transpower story shows that safety is not a thing you manage directly, in isolation. It's an outcome of how work is designed, how people relate to each other, and whether the conditions exist for people to do their jobs well.

When those conditions are missing, when people are exhausted, under-resourced, blamed, or shut out of decision-making, safety suffers. Not because people don't care, but because the system is working against them.

Conversation is how you build shared understanding of those systemic issues. Not only so you can fix them for people, but so you can work on them together, create something everyone can commit to. It's how both sides see what the other sees, how constraints become discussable rather than hidden, and how solutions emerge from joint sensemaking rather than being imposed from above.

What safety conversations are

The Transpower story shows what becomes possible when conversation is real. But much of what we call "safety conversations" today aren't real at all.

Many organisations have created safety conversation programs with a genuine intent to make safety visible, to show that leaders care, and to get people into the field. But over time, even well-designed programs drift into ritual. The leader walks the site, asking predetermined questions to hit their monthly target, while the worker knows exactly what to say to make it end quickly. Everyone plays their part and it looks like conversation, but underneath, it's little more than a box-ticking exercise.

So, what made the Transpower conversation different?

The leaders didn't arrive with a checklist. They didn't know what they would hear. They asked open questions they were curious to find the answers to, and then, they waited. When the painters hesitated, leaders didn't fill the silence or redirect. When answers implicated leadership decisions, Transpower's leaders didn't defend; they just listened.

It didn't follow a neat conversation process with steps for connection, asking questions, giving feedback, saying thank you and moving on. There was no neat conclusion at the end of the meeting either. What did emerge was messy, uncomfortable, and incomplete, but it was also real, and that's what mattered.

This is what genuine safety conversations look like in practice: uncertain, emergent, and requiring leaders to share control of where the conversation goes.

> Programs fade, initiatives lose momentum, and campaigns run their course, but conversation – when it's real – changes the relational ground beneath everything else.

When conversation is real – when people can finally name what has been unspoken – something powerful happens. For years, the delays, quality problems, and injuries had been treated as individual failures of the tower painters, put down to lack of motivation, inadequate skill, and resistance to change. Yet when the conversation finally happened, leaders stopped seeing the painters as problems to be managed and started seeing them as people navigating impossible conditions. The painters stopped protecting themselves and started contributing. In the process, they became partners.

Once people could speak honestly and be heard honestly, responsibility emerged naturally. Because people were finally treated as responsible, agency and pride returned. The work became safer because the work became more human.

Programs fade, initiatives lose momentum, and campaigns run their course, but conversation – when it's real – changes the relational ground beneath everything else.

The table below shows, at a glance, what safety conversations are and what they are not.

What safety conversations are not	**What safety conversations are**
Audits in disguise – designed to verify compliance and count activity.	Moments of discovery – trying to understand how work happens.
Structured performances – following a script, tidy, predictable.	Emergent encounters – open, responsive, shaped by what people bring.
Rule-checking – comparing behaviour to procedure.	Sensemaking – exploring what helps or hinders good work.
Top-down – reinforcing hierarchy and control.	Two-way – sharing ownership, insight, and responsibility.
Measurement-driven – judged by the number completed.	Meaning-driven – valued for what was learned and changed.
Seeking certainty – neat stories, clear causes, fast fixes.	Inviting ambiguity – honest, messy, and revealing of reality.

Your next conversation

You don't need to read this entire book before you change something. Your next conversation with someone about their work, whether you call it a safety conversation or not, is an opportunity. You can show up checking, verifying, measuring, and performing, or you can show up curious, present, and genuinely interested in understanding how work happens. You can ask questions you already know the answers to, or you can ask questions you don't. You can listen for compliance, or you can listen for insight.

Transpower's tower-painting program didn't transform because people suddenly cared more or tried harder. It transformed because the conversation finally created space for partnership. Leaders stopped arriving with solutions and started exploring constraints together. Painters stopped defending their work and started describing it openly. Both sides brought what the other alone couldn't see.

That didn't require special training, a new framework, or organisational permission. It required curiosity, humility, and the willingness to be changed by what was heard. It required stepping into "we".

That's available to you right now, in your next conversation. The question isn't whether your people have the answers (they do, and so do you). The question is whether you're ready to work on them together, to build shared understanding before rushing to solutions, and to shape what's possible as partners, not as manager and managed.

Your next conversation is an opportunity to choose between "How do I get you to ...?" or "How do we improve ...?"

Choose the second question. Build the "we".

CHAPTER 2

When Organisations Go Deaf

The day before the Deepwater Horizon exploded, four senior executives from BP and Transocean helicoptered onto the oil rig. Part of the purpose of their visit was to make upper management more visible to workers. There were also specific safety reasons for being there. The Deepwater Horizon had achieved seven years without a lost-time injury, and the visitors wanted to congratulate the crew on the milestone, share lessons, and see whether any best practices could be transferred across the fleet.

Each executive came with a particular focus. One wanted to check how the rig was addressing a slip hazard recently identified on another installation. Another inspected fall protection harnesses, checking whether their tags were up to date. All of them spoke repeatedly about an ongoing campaign to reduce hand injuries and dropped objects; a key theme across both organisations.

They walked the decks, inspected lockers, checked tags and signs, and commended the crew for spotless housekeeping. They asked about toolbox talks, near-miss reporting, and the "Stop Work Authority". Everything looked as it should, and everyone had the right answers. The executives were engaged, observant, and sincere.

Beneath the surface, though, the well was becoming unstable. In the drilling shack, the crew were debating confusing test results that hinted at a dangerous pressure build-up. Something was wrong, but no one fully grasped it. People felt uneasy – the data did not sit comfortably – and the results did not align with expectations. To those closest to the work, the signals weren't weak; they were confusing, contested, and unresolved. Yet the tension never became central to the visiting leaders' conversations. They were not ignoring warning signs; they simply didn't recognise them as such. The leaders encountered fragments of the difficulty without recognising their significance. In any case, they were there to talk about safety, not to wrestle with the well.

After the walkaround, they gathered the crew for a celebration: seven years lost-time-injury-free. There were photographs, cake, and applause. One of the leaders thanked everyone for their commitment and reminded them to "stay safe".

Seven hours later, the rig exploded. Eleven people died.

What the Deepwater Horizon story reveals is a failure of relationship, where the executives and the drilling crew occupied the same rig but lived in different realities. Leadership saw compliance and order, while the crew felt uncertainty and pressure. There was no "we" strong enough to bridge that gap, and no relationship that could carry difficult truths upward, or from one reality to the next, before they became catastrophic. When organisations split into "us" (leadership, assurance, oversight) and "them" (operations, frontline, the work), the distance between these worlds doesn't just create information problems, it creates relational fracture. And when the relationship fractures, the organisation can't understand itself.

Everyone on that rig was doing what the system expected – managing safety through inspection, compliance, and visible order. The visiting executives were following an inherited model of safety that focused on slips, PPE, housekeeping, and behavioural markers. What got measured got managed, but it wasn't hearing what mattered most.

Empathy for the senior leaders

Imagine sitting at the top of BP or Transocean. You carry ultimate responsibility for the safe operation of multiple offshore oil platforms. These are among the most advanced machines ever built, operating in hostile environments, under global scrutiny, with enormous financial, human, and ecological risk.

You are not responsible for one rig, but for many – twenty, thirty. The technical detail exceeds any one person's capacity. The cues that matter most (subtle unease, shifting pressures, operational discomfort) do not travel easily across organisational layers. As those cues move upward, they are attenuated. Each layer filters, translates, and smooths what it receives, until what arrives feels weak, abstract, or disconnected from the work itself. You can't feel the behaviour of a well through paperwork.

But there is little room for doubt, no space for visible disorder, and certainly no acceptance for accidents. You must reassure investors, regulators, governments, communities, and perhaps yourself most of all. So, how do you know safety is present?

You look for what can travel – what can be measured, compared, audited, aggregated, and reported across platforms. Measures that are real, objective, verifiable, and reliable, such as tidy decks, PPE compliance, training records and completed checklists, procedures that are reviewed and campaigns that are rolled out, green lights on dashboards, and a lost-time injury rate sitting at zero.

These signals can make the journey from a rig in the Gulf of Mexico to a boardroom in London or Houston. They are the signals your role is designed to receive. What reaches you becomes what you understand, what you understand becomes what you act on, and what you act on becomes what the organisation learns to prioritise.

Over time, the system shapes its own field of vision. It rewards attention to what can be made orderly and visible, not necessarily to what is most consequential.

And here's the insidious part: the very systems designed to give you control prevent you from building the relationships that would let you see reality more clearly. Every dashboard that promises visibility creates distance. Every layer of reporting that should inform you filters out the human texture that would help you understand.

The senior leaders who walked Deepwater Horizon the day before it exploded were not indifferent or uncaring. They were responding exactly as the organisational architecture required: they inspected what could be inspected; they saw what the system had trained them to see; they were close enough to verify order, yet too far to sense the risk unfolding beneath their feet.

Staying in contact

The signals that matter most – unease, hesitation, pressure, workarounds, emerging solutions – rarely travel far because they don't fit the channels designed to carry other kinds of information.

Dashboards can't feel the mood on a job, audits can't register the anxiety that precedes an incident, and KPIs can't detect when relationships are straining under pressure.

Data systems capture what's measurable by turning experience into numbers, ambiguity into categories, and reality into analytical statements. What they can't do is close the relational distance between the people making decisions and the people navigating the consequences. They can't build the trust required for difficult truths to travel, and they can't help leaders understand not just *what* is happening, but *why* it's happening, what it costs, and what it means.

So, organisations drift, slowly but steadily. The language of actual work becomes thinner as it travels upward. Leaders inherit proxies instead of insight, workers learn which truths fit the form and which don't, and with it, the us/them fracture deepens.

> This is the paradox leaders face: the more you try to see through control, the less you see. The more you try to know through systems, the less you understand through relationship. And the less you understand, the more you reach for control. The cycle reinforces itself.

The organisational disconnection is not solved by more tools or more controls. Those are the very mechanisms that created the distance in the first place. Breaking this cycle requires something most leadership frameworks don't prepare you for: giving up the illusion of control to gain genuine understanding.

What restores contact is conversation, not as another system to implement, but as a relational practice that closes the us/them distance. When leaders genuinely listen to frontline employees, when people can speak honestly without fear, when sensemaking happens together rather than separately, then the organisation can begin to see itself clearly again.

Which brings it back to you, face to face with someone doing the work, asking, How do we resist the drift towards us/them? How do we show up as partners? How do we create “we” instead of maintaining separation?

The answer isn’t a new technique or process. It’s about how you show up, the qualities you bring, the stance you take, and the relationship you create through how you listen and respond. That’s the inner work we turn to next.

CHAPTER 3

Conversations Beyond Scripts

"Can you tell me about a time when your work was difficult?"

For a moment, the group of construction workers just stared at me, puzzled, curious, unsure. Then one of them broke the silence. "It's the tools," he said. "We don't have enough of them."

My fear was materialising that the session would become an opinion fest, but I'd come prepared. "That sounds interesting. Tell me about a time when that made things hard."

"Well ... yesterday. The storeman told me he'd lent the last one to Bob, who was on the other structure. I spent forty-five minutes looking for him. When I finally found Bob, he'd already lent it to someone else."

Suddenly, the stories came out thick and fast – tools being hidden to keep them close by, tradespeople buying their own equipment because they couldn't trust the system, borrowing from rival contractors and trading favours in return ... An economy of workarounds had formed, creating solutions that no audit, report, or observation had ever noticed.

I hadn't gone in with a survey to complete or a checklist to verify. I wanted to understand their world. One curious question opened a door, and what followed came from how I showed up being interested, unhurried, and willing to hear what mattered to them.

This is the challenge every safety conversation faces. You don't control how the other person experiences you, what they feel able to say, or where the conversation might lead. History, hierarchy, and pressure walk into the room with you. Time is limited, so what matters most often arrives sideways, disguised as complaints, such as, "The mattress at camp is hard." "They cancelled the Christmas party." In the moment, these sound trivial, but later, you realise they were signals. And when conversation matters most, the usual tools of scripts, predetermined questions and checklists offer little to hold on to.

What you can hold on to is how you show up. When outcomes are uncertain and control is limited, the qualities you bring become the most reliable anchor. From the assumptions you carry into the conversation, to the discomfort you can tolerate, or the space you create simply by how you listen, respond, and stay, all shape whether curiosity is real or performative, whether honesty feels possible or risky, and whether the conversation opens or quietly closes down.

When I first started having conversations with frontline employees about their work, I thought the challenge was external. I focused on finding the right questions, applying rapport-building frameworks, and guiding conversations through active listening. I treated conversation as a technical task – something you could improve by learning better techniques.

However, over time I realised that the quality of a conversation depended less on what I asked and more on what I brought into it. My assumptions about people, my discomfort with silence, my urge to fix or explain, my need to appear competent – all of this shaped how I listened, what I noticed, and what I allowed into the conversation. All of this was present before I said a word.

This chapter is about that inner work or the inner conditions that shape whether curiosity is real or performative, whether listening is open or selective, whether silence feels spacious or threatening.

Whether you are learning how work happens, appreciating what is already working, exploring new possibilities, inviting accountability, or repairing trust, the same inner ground is required.

The practices that follow aren't techniques to master, but qualities to cultivate. They are ways of showing up that create the conditions where truth can be spoken.

Three qualities that shape conversations

I've learnt that there are three critical qualities that shape safety conversations:

- Curiosity
- Compassion
- Courage

These are ways of being that create the conditions where truth can be spoken. Think of them as three overlapping circles: curiosity lets you see what's there; compassion helps you stay with what you hear without fixing it; and courage allows you to name what you encounter, even when it's uncomfortable.

Together, they create something most safety conversations lack, which is a relational ground stable enough for honesty.

Let's look at what each one looks like in practice.

The quality of a conversation depended less on what I asked and more on what I brought into it.

Listening with curiosity

I thought I knew about manual handling. I'd read the research, seen the training videos, and I understood the biomechanics. So, when a kitchen worker mentioned the "manual-handling training", as one of the things that had shaped the workplace, I almost moved on. But something made me pause. "What made it good?" I asked.

What followed wasn't about lifting technique at all. It was about asking for help. The facilitator had reframed dependency on others as *professionalism*. One phrase – "That's when you ask for help" – had changed an entire team's culture.

I would have missed all of it if I'd trusted what I thought I knew.

Curiosity is a refusal to let your technical knowledge replace someone's lived experience of work. It's noticing when you think you already know the answer and choosing to ask anyway. Most of us enter conversations with a plan – we have questions to ask, agendas to cover, forms to complete – but the trouble starts when the plan becomes more important than the person in front of us.

Meaningful safety conversations often begin exactly when we're tempted to move on. The employee gives a neat answer, everything sounds like "nothing here to look at", so we feel ready to go to the next question.

But if you listen closely, there is often something hiding inside that neat answer, whether it's a phrase that sounds slightly rehearsed, a pause that lingers a fraction too long, a tiny shrug, a glance sideways, a comment that doesn't quite match the expression on their face ...

Listening with curiosity means treating those small signals as invitations. So, instead of following the form, you follow the conversation.

Ask things like, "You said, 'we manage'. What does that look like today?" Or admit what you don't know; for example, "I don't think I understand what Monday morning is like for you. Tell me about it." Or pick up on the small signals; for example, "You paused just then. What were you thinking?"

This signals your interest, that you want to understand, that you take your conversation partner seriously, and that they are important. In doing so, it is allowing their story to stretch out enough for reality to appear.

Most of what shapes how work happens isn't written down anywhere. It lives in relationships, judgements, and quiet adjustments people make on the fly. It lives in the pressures that wax and wane, the social dynamics of a crew, the way two people always swap a task because they trust each other's way of doing it. If we only listen for what fits our checklist, we will only ever hear the part of the story that already fits the system.

Curiosity is about having fewer assumptions. It is the willingness to admit that, however many times you have seen this job done, you have never seen it through this person's eyes on this day.

Compassion in response

Curiosity opens the door, but it's not enough. I learned this the hard way.

The maintenance manager slammed his hand on the table. "This," he said, "sitting here with you while I have no idea what's happening in my workshop."

I had two choices. I could explain why these conversations matter, defend my process, redirect to safer topics, or I could stay with his frustration. "It sounds like there's a lot on your desk," I said.

What followed wasn't an answer but a release. Corporate pressure ... Parts arriving late ... Contractors he couldn't control ... Employees he felt responsible for but struggled to support ... The sheer weight of holding it all alone ...

When he finally paused, I had an overwhelming urge to reassure him, to tell him it would be okay, to offer solutions and assure him that our time together was worthwhile. Anything to reduce the intensity in the room. But that urge was about my comfort, not his needs – he didn't need reassurance, he needed to be heard – so, I stayed quiet and let him keep going.

People rarely struggle because they don't care about safety. They struggle because the way we have designed work can make good performance harder than it needs to be. When someone tells you about a difficult part of the job, they're offering you more than data. They are letting you into a small part of what the work asks of them, such as how much effort it takes, how much frustration they swallow, and how much risk they carry on behalf of the organisation.

If we respond by correcting, explaining, or minimising, we send a strong signal that their experience doesn't really count.

Compassion means letting their world matter. This isn't just intellectually understanding their constraints but feeling the weight of what work asks of them. It means treating what they tell you as a perspective the system needs to hear, and not a whinge.

In practice, compassion may sound like:

- "That sounds exhausting. How long has it been like that?"
- "What do you have to trade off to make that work?"
- "What would make this easier for you to do well?"

And then staying with the answer, even when it implicates the system you're part of. Even when fixing it isn't within your power or when all you can offer is understanding.

Think back to the Transpower tower painters. Understanding their experience made the standards more achievable. It grounded the organisation in what the work asked of people. When their world mattered, better solutions appeared. Rather than weakening accountability, compassion made it workable.

In such conversations, you will hear about layouts that demand too much, equipment that doesn't match the workflow, procedures that work on paper but not in practice, and informal workarounds that are faster, better, and sometimes safer than the official methods.

The temptation is to jump straight to fixing. Sometimes that's necessary, but if we fix too quickly, we miss the meaning of what we've just heard. We miss the chance to understand how the system lives in people, such as where it supports, where it confuses, where it burdens, and where it protects.

The courage to stay

Curiosity and compassion create openness. But openness isn't always comfortable. Sometimes what people share is confronting. Sometimes it implicates you, your decisions, or your organisation. It might demand something from you that you're not sure you can give.

That's when courage becomes necessary.

"Why should I tell you anything?" the stores person snapped. "Two years ago, another consultant came here, asked a bunch of questions about my work, my ideas. I never heard back from him. Never saw a single change from all that. So why should I talk with you?"

For a moment I felt the impulse to defend myself, to explain how I was different, to promise that this time would be different. Every instinct said, *Smooth this over, move on, find someone more cooperative.*

Instead, I said, "Okay. Tell me about that experience then. Who was it? What did they ask? What was promised?"

> Staying in the conversation when it is tense is how we honour the risk people take when they speak honestly.

For some reason, she engaged. She told me what she'd shared back then, from the problems she'd raised, to the ideas she'd offered, how hopeful she'd been that something might finally shift. Then she described the slow realisation that nothing was coming. She described the disappointment, the feeling of being used, and the sense that speaking up was a waste of breath.

When she finished, there was silence. I didn't fill it.

Eventually, she asked, "So what are you going to do with what I tell you?"

"I honestly don't know yet," I said. "But I can promise I won't disappear. Even if the answer is 'we can't change that right now', you'll hear back from me."

She studied my face for a moment, then she started talking about the real issues.

Moments like this test your willingness to stay. They also reveal the cost of conversations that were never closed, honoured, or returned to.

Safety conversations can be uncomfortable. It's upsetting to hear how people are ridiculed when they've raised an issue, or that putting something into the reporting system generates little more than an automatic email saying, *This has been filed for statistical purposes.*

Sometimes you hear about dangerous practices. Sometimes you stumble across systemic negligence that goes all the way to the top, and sometimes you wish people hadn't told you certain things.

When it's confronting to hear these things, or it demands something uncomfortable from us, we are inclined to change the subject, explain, give a promise that this time will be different, or say, "Yes, but ...".

Staying when it gets uncomfortable is a different move. It means letting the tension stay on the table long enough for it to change us.

Try phrases like:

- "That's hard to hear, but I'm glad you said it. Tell me more."
- "If that's true, what does it mean we need to do differently?"
- "I'm part of the reason it's like this. Let's talk about that."

Most of the courage needed in safety conversations is small, ordinary, and demanding. It takes courage to say:

- "I don't know."
- "I may be wrong."
- "I hadn't seen it that way."
- "This is unsafe."
- "This isn't working."

When we say these things from a place of honesty and care, rather than from a desire to sound aligned with whatever standard is fashionable, they become invitations rather than threats, and they open space for others to be honest too.

Courage in conversation often looks like:

- asking a second question instead of closing the topic
- noticing hesitation and pausing rather than pushing forward
- saying “this is hard” without blaming anyone
- staying silent, letting the words sink in, giving space for the story to go deeper
- holding back our clever idea so someone else can offer theirs.

Staying in the conversation when it is tense is how we honour the risk people take when they speak honestly. If we step away as soon as things get awkward, we train people not to bring us anything that might matter.

Finding your stance

Every conversation carries a set of orientation questions beneath it. These are not questions for the other person, but questions for you. Think about whether you are there to:

- diagnose or discover
- audit or accompany
- control or be curious
- be an expert, or to learn from those closest to the work?

These questions aren’t about which stance is “right”. They’re about noticing which stance you’re actually in because you can’t show up with curiosity, compassion, and courage if you haven’t first noticed you’re showing up with judgement, impatience, or certainty.

Your stance shapes what you notice, what you follow, what you ignore, and what becomes possible. A genuine conversation is two or more people exploring something together without already knowing where it will lead. Such inquiry needs freedom to speak, to reveal, to think aloud, to be more human than a job title. The moment we try to persuade, correct, or prove ourselves right, the conversation begins to shrink.

Signal or noise?

Sometimes what makes conversations difficult isn't conflict or emotion, but uncertainty about whether what we're hearing matters at all. Is it relevant for safety when someone says:

- "The mattress at camp is so hard. I barely sleep."
- "They pulled the plug on the Christmas party this year."
- "We're not getting the company uniforms because we're contractors."

None of these statements arrived with a label attached. They didn't announce themselves as safety issues, they didn't sound like hazards, and they didn't come wrapped in the language of risk. They sound like complaints, or observations, or passing remarks made over coffee, in the crib room, on the way to the truck.

And yet, each one left a question hanging in the air. Is this just a gripe? Is it about comfort, fairness, morale? Is it resistance to change? Is it background noise in a busy system? Or is something else being spoken, sideways?

Take the mattress comment, for example. It could be a comfort complaint from someone who likes softer beds, but perhaps it's a fatigue risk with chronic poor sleep affecting alertness and decision-making?

Or the Christmas party. It could be a cost-cutting observation noting that budgets are tight. Or perhaps it's a morale indicator with people feeling that the company doesn't value them?

Instead of deciding what a comment means, stay curious about what it *might* mean. Follow the thread a bit further. "Tell me more. How is the mattress issue impacting your work?" Often, one more question reveals whether there's depth underneath.

The most important information rarely comes neatly packaged. It arrives as asides, casual mentions, or humour that carries an edge. Learning to recognise this requires staying attuned to what's beneath the surface.

The judgement whether to treat what we're hearing as noise or as a signal can't be automated. It can't be reduced to a rule, and it rarely feels clean. What matters here is whether we are willing to stay curious long enough to find out what a comment might be pointing towards, rather than closing it down because it doesn't sound serious enough. Only after the fact do we get to say, "That was a signal," or "That was noise." In the moment, all we have is a conversation, and the choice of whether to listen long enough for meaning to emerge.

From scripts to landscapes

By now you might be thinking, *This sounds messy. How do I know where to go? What if I ask about tools and they want to talk about barbecues?*

Good. That means you're starting to see the limitation of scripts.

I once started a conversation with an electrical linesworker on a site where I'd been asked to gather frontline ideas for improvement. I opened with a simple question: “If you had $50,000 to improve work around here, how would you spend it?”

He paused for a moment, then said, “I’d probably organise a big barbecue.”

It wasn’t the answer I expected. It sounded almost flippant. Was he not taking the question seriously? Was he more interested in food than fixing the job? But instead of dismissing it, I stayed curious. “How would that improve work?”

He shrugged gently. “Team spirit’s down the drain at the moment because of what’s going on with the restructure. People are tired and disconnected. That’s what needs fixing first.”

I came looking for technical fixes, and he pointed to human need. The conversation followed what mattered to him, and in doing so, revealed what the system most needed to hear. If I had followed a checklist with predetermined questions, or a conversation process with a start, middle and end, it’d be unlikely to uncover what mattered.

It may be helpful to think of conversations as a landscape with different regions, each with its own character and purpose. A conversation that begins with learning how work happens might reveal something worth appreciating, which opens space for exploring what could be different. What matters more than a script to follow is noticing where you are in the conversation. Think about moving responsively, following what emerges, and trusting that the conversation will show you what it needs.

Good conversationalists don’t follow a process mechanically, they read the situation, they notice when the energy shifts, when someone hesitates, when a question lands differently than expected, and when the conversation opens or contracts.

Gradually, you’ll develop a sense for when to stay in one “region” and when to follow the conversation somewhere else.

You'll notice when understanding isn't enough and action needs discussing (accountability). You'll feel when the ground between you needs attention before the conversation can go further (connection, or restoration).

The chapters that follow explore six types of conversations: connection, learning, appreciating, exploring possibility, inviting accountability, and restoring trust. Each has its own purpose, its own patterns, and its own challenges.

But all of them rest on this same foundation: your capacity to show up with curiosity, compassion, and courage. Without that inner ground, the techniques in later chapters won't help. With it, you won't need as many techniques as you think.

Your next conversation is an opportunity to practise. Not to get it perfect, but to notice and think, *When am I curious? When am I compassionate? When am I courageous? And where do I have room to grow?*

The quality of that next conversation won't depend on following steps but on how you show up, whether you arrive checking or exploring, whether you listen for compliance or insight, and whether you stay when things get difficult, or you smooth them over.

That choice is always available to you. In every conversation.

PART TWO

The Six Conversation Types

CHAPTER 4

Connection

I felt completely out of place as I arrived at a construction site to talk to employees about their work. It was in south-central Queensland, not long after I had moved to Australia in 2011. I had just finished my studies, and I was full of theory, ideas, and enthusiasm. I was now about to "engage the workforce".

This was my first real test. My manager had committed me to a flagship construction project. The client was expecting something meaningful – preferably something impressive – and I was supposed to deliver it.

When I arrived, the difference between me and the people I was supposed to talk with hit me immediately. They were the classic Queensland construction crew – blokes who were tanned, with bushy beards, faded and thinned orange shirts from years of use, tattoos winding up their forearms. It was like a bikie gang in PPE. And then there was me – Swedish, pale, tall and scrawny, freshly pressed in a brand-new hi-vis shirt that still had creases from the packaging, a hard hat so shiny it could have doubled as a mirror.

I had theories about organisational learning and ideas about human factors. I had read research papers and studied emerging safety approaches. What I didn't have was any standing with these people, any credibility, or any reason for them to take me seriously. And I needed them to talk. Not to perform for me, not to humour the kid from head office, but to open up and spill the beans about how work happened on site.

That evening, sitting in the camp canteen with a tray of food and a knot in my stomach, one thought kept looping: *How on earth am I supposed to connect with these people? I have nothing in common with them.*

The next morning, sitting in front of the group, I decided to name it. I took a deep breath and said, "Good morning. My name is Daniel. I work in safety, in head office in Brisbane. I'm new to this company and, as you can probably tell, I'm not from here. I'm from Sweden, so that explains the accent. All of which means that I have absolutely no idea what it's like to work here on site."

There was a beat of silence. Someone said, "None of us do, mate." Everyone laughed. The ice broke and the conversation began.

In that moment I realised that connection doesn't come from similarity, but from honesty. And, more importantly, connection is what makes good conversation possible.

Why connection matters

What happens when an outsider walks onto a site to talk about safety? The people you want to speak with make micro-assessments in the first thirty seconds. They're reading:

- who you are, really

- why you're there
- what you want from them
- whether they can trust you with the truth
- if you're on the same side.

These assessments happen quickly, often beneath conscious awareness, shaping what follows. In safety conversations, this assessment carries extra weight. Employees likely have memories of being questioned, judged, audited, corrected, and disciplined. They've learned to be careful about what they reveal and to whom. They're attuned to whether someone wants to learn or merely inspect.

Connection is what makes honesty possible. When it's present, people take small risks with what they share. They describe the parts of work that don't sit neatly inside procedures. They name what's difficult. When connection is absent, they might perform an acceptable image rather than speak their truth. So, how you respond matters.

This chapter is about how that connection is formed, through how we arrive, how we relate, and how we create enough space for real talk to happen. Before we can learn, appreciate, or commit to a shared future, connection must be present.

Connection happens through three movements that build on each other:

- Presence: People sense you're here (not performing, not rushing).
- Permission: They sense it's safe to speak (you're not judging).
- Partnership: They sense their input matters (they shape what happens next).

Each one builds on the previous. You can't create permission without presence. You can't create partnership without permission or presence.

Let's explore each.

Presence: How you arrive

The first signal people receive about you is not your introduction, or your question, but your presence.

- Do you arrive quickly or slowly?
- Are you scanning for wrongdoers or meeting people?
- Is your mind in the room or back in your inbox?
- Are you there to reach an "interaction quota", or to learn?

When I'm on site, I assume people want to talk with me. That assumption shifts me from inspecting to meeting. I slow down, make eye contact, and smile, even when I feel uncertain. I greet people by name if I know them or ask if I don't. These small gestures communicate that I am a guest entering someone else's world of work, and we will take the next steps together.

Presence is practised through slowing down. Speed tends to crowd out connection, and rushing tells people that this moment doesn't really matter. Slowing down (arriving unhurried, giving space for silence, putting away your phone, noticing what's happening in the room) signals the opposite.

It also means paying attention and noticing people. How they hold themselves, whether they're comfortable or guarded, what the energy feels like. These observations are information about whether connection is forming or whether you need to adjust.

These are recalibrations that help you become genuinely present rather than merely physically present. Presence is a choice you make before you speak. It says, "I'm here, for this conversation, to hear what you have to say."

Permission: Making space for honesty

I once sat in on a safety toolbox talk between a supervisor and his team. The supervisor asked, "Any safety concerns? Nope, all good." The supervisor made a note and moved on.

After he left, I asked one of the team members, "What would you change about how this work is set up?"

"Mate, where do I start?" He described significant concerns he'd been carrying for weeks.

"Why didn't you mention those earlier?"

"What's the point? Last time someone raised something, they got a lecture about following the procedure. Easier to just say 'all good' and get on with it."

Permission to talk freely doesn't come from a policy or poster. It comes from someone, and preferably from the person in front of them. People speak freely when they sense three things:

They won't be judged.

They won't be punished.

They won't be made to look foolish.

You offer permission when you:

- acknowledge your limits
- share a little vulnerability
- speak as a person, not a role
- give them choice in how the conversation proceeds.

For example: "I don't know the job the way you do, so I'll be relying on you to help me understand."

This removes the tension that most safety conversations carry. It signals that you're not under review, and your experience matters here.

Permission grows when you ask real questions driven by genuine curiosity, such as:

- "What makes this part of the job tricky?"
- "What would you change if you could?"
- "How do you know when something isn't right?"

Real questions say, "I am here to understand." They invite people to think aloud rather than perform correctness. They make space for ambiguity, uncertainty, and honesty.

When people sense that they have permission to speak freely, their bodies relax, their answers get longer, they start offering examples unprompted. The performance drops away and the real conversation begins.

Partnership: Shaping the conversation together

Most safety conversations carry an implicit power imbalance: manager and worker, safety and operations, assessor and assessed. Partnership is the antidote to that dynamic.

I once opened a conversation by asking, "I need to understand how the handover process works. Where should we start?"

The crew looked at each other, surprised. One said, "You're asking us?"

"You do it every day. I've never done it once. So, yes, I'm asking you." That small shift of acknowledging their expertise and giving them agency over where we began shaped what followed. Instead of answering my questions, they started teaching me, and instead of being subjects of inquiry, they became guides.

Partnership sounds like:

- "What is on your mind today?"
- "What are you working on at the moment?"
- "What is making the job easier or harder right now?"
- "Is there something you think we should understand better?"

These questions give people room to choose where to begin. They signal that the conversation is ours – you have agency here too – and what matters to both of us shapes where we go next.

This isn't about abandoning your purpose. You may have specific topics you need to explore, but partnership means starting where they are, not where you need to end up. Trust that the conversation will get you there.

Here's what that shift sounds like in practice:

Without partnership	With partnership
"I need to ask you about the incident yesterday."	"I'm trying to understand what happened yesterday. Where would be helpful to start?"
"Walk me through your prestart checklist."	"Help me understand what you're thinking about before you start work."
"Why aren't you using the approved lifting device?"	"I noticed you're using a different method. Walk me through what you do."
"Here's the new process. Any questions?"	"Here's what we're thinking. What are we missing from your perspective?"

Every conversation has threads – moments of energy, emotion, or insight – and we need to follow those threads. For example:

- "You frowned when you said that. What's happening there?"
- "You mentioned pressure. Tell me more about that."

These moves show you're paying attention to their experience, not just your agenda. Start with one of the topics they offer up, and trust deepens. The harder, more important topics usually surface on their own once the relationship feels trustworthy.

Partnership turns the conversation from something being done to someone, into something being done with them. It transforms the power dynamic without erasing the hierarchy. The difference in roles remains, but the dignity is shared.

How connection shows itself

You can feel when connection forms. Not because you've followed a formula, but because something shifts in the room.

I was once talking with a freight crew about what made their work difficult. For the first ten minutes, answers were polite and generic. "Yeah, it's busy." "We manage." "Could always use more time." Then someone mentioned an equipment issue that had been frustrating them for months. As he spoke, his shoulders dropped. He leaned forward, and the careful performance fell away. What emerged was the real frustration, the real problem.

Another crew member jumped in, "Yes! The frustrating thing is that we gave them feedback on that design before they decided to put it in, and here we are ..."

A third person added their experience. The conversation accelerated. Someone made a joke, and everyone laughed.

I had asked the same types of questions throughout, but something had shifted. They stopped performing answers and started thinking aloud. The *connection* was there.

Look out for these subtle shifts:

- Shoulders drop, arms uncross, people start to mirror each other's body language.
- Someone who was standing settles their weight.
- Voices soften and humour appears.
- The pace slows naturally.
- Stories begin to arrive, unprompted.

These tell you that connection is forming. Not perfectly, necessarily, but sufficiently for truth to begin travelling. But connection alone isn't the destination – it's the foundation. Once it's there, the question becomes: What does this moment need?

What does this moment need?

Connection creates the ground, so what do you build on that ground? That depends on what the moment is asking for.

Sometimes the answer is clear:

- Someone just had a near miss. They probably need space to make sense of what happened before you move to what should happen next.
- You've asked people to change a practice. They'll need to understand the pressure or constraint before they can explore how to respond.
- A relationship is strained after a difficult event. Repair needs to happen before learning can resume.

- Work is going well and people are quietly doing excellent things. This is the moment to notice and name what's working.

Often, the conversation itself will reveal what it needs, as you move through it. So, before stepping into a conversation, pause and ask yourself, "What does this moment need?"

Understanding the bigger landscape of where the conversation might take you helps you recognise where you are and what it offers. Think of these not as separate conversation types to choose from, but as "regions" you might move through in a single conversation. You might start with learning (understanding how work happens), which reveals something worth appreciating (what's working well), which opens space for possibility (what could be different), which requires accountability (committing to action), and if things have been strained, you might need restoration first (repairing the ground).

Learning creates understanding. You discover how work is done, what people navigate, and where the system helps or hinders. Chapter 5 shows how to move beyond checklists into genuine discovery.

Appreciation creates confidence. When you notice what people bring and what already works, you strengthen the conditions that allow work to thrive. Chapter 6 explores how to see and speak about the enabling capacity that's often invisible.

Possibility conversations help people imagine what could be different and explore ideas that haven't yet found a place in the system. They can turn workarounds into innovations. Chapter 7 explores this territory.

Accountability conversations connect expectations to meaning, identity, and care for others. Not through pressure or consequences, but through invitation. Chapter 8 shows how responsibility is invited rather than enforced.

Restorative conversations help people find their way back to working together with trust after strain, conflict, or harm. Chapter 9 shows what becomes possible when we attend to rupture.

The point isn't to decide which conversation type you're having. It's to notice where you are and respond to what the moment needs.

When connection doesn't form

Sometimes, despite your best efforts, connection doesn't happen. The person across from you has been burned too many times, or they're carrying something you can't see. Perhaps your role makes genuine connection impossible in this moment, and that's okay – you can't force connection. What you can do is:

- Acknowledge it: "I'm sensing this conversation isn't landing well. Is this not a good time?"
- Give them control: "Would it be better if we talked about something else first? Or if I came back later?"
- Respect the boundary: "I appreciate you giving me some time anyway."

Sometimes the best thing you can do for connection is stop trying to force it and let the person keep their ground.

Why connection matters for the whole organisation

Connection is the prerequisite for every other conversation type in this book. Without connection, people default to performance. They give you the version of the story that sounds most acceptable, looks most compliant, or requires the least vulnerability.

The conversation may look fine on the surface, but underneath, no real information moves.

> Connection isn't built once. It has to be re-established, especially across hierarchy and power differences.

Each conversation asks you to establish it anew, by showing up with the same qualities that made it possible before.

Every time you slow down, make eye contact, and show you're actually interested, you make it a little safer for truth to move.

What follows in the next chapters assumes connection is already there. Without it, none of the other conversation types work.

CHAPTER 5

Learning Conversations

The purpose of learning conversations is simple: to understand how people make work succeed and avoid failure in real conditions, and to see how the system lives in day-to-day practice. That means seeing work through other people's eyes, from what they're trying to achieve, to what makes their work possible, what gets in the way, and how they adapt when conditions don't match the plan.

It also means recognising that your view of the work – shaped by your role, where you're based, and responsibilities – probably differs from theirs. Are you willing to let their perspective challenge yours? Are you open to discovering that the work is harder, messier, or more intelligent than you realised?

Learning conversations put the three core qualities from Chapter 3 into practice. Curiosity drives us to understand work as it happens. Compassion helps us stay with difficulty. Courage allows us to hear what's uncomfortable.

Learning conversations help you see where the system helps and where it hinders, what people know that procedures don't capture, and what would make work safer and better. This chapter shows you how to move from surface compliance to genuine discovery.

Understanding how work happens

"Understanding work" can be challenging. Work has depth, so what you see on the surface – the steps, the tools, the procedures – is only part of the story. Beneath the visible work sits another layer: the pressures, the competing goals, and the constraints that shape how work unfolds. And beneath that sits the intelligence people bring, the adaptations, the trade-offs, workarounds, and judgement that keep things moving when conditions don't match the plan.

Think of these as three layers of understanding, each one revealing something the layer above conceals:

Layer 1: The work itself

What people do, the tools they use, the sequence of steps, the environment they work in. This is the visible, tangible work.

Layer 2: The pressures and goals

What drives the work, what shapes trade-offs, what people are trying to achieve or avoid. This is where competing priorities collide.

Layer 3: How people adapt

The intelligence people bring, the adjustments they make, the informal systems that hold things together. This is where expertise lives.

Learning conversations move through these layers, from surface to depth.

Layer 1: The work itself

Layer 1 is the visible, tangible work made up of the tools, materials, steps, controls, and the flow of the task as it unfolds. This is where work plans meet reality, and where people's bodies, tools, and time interact.

When you're learning about the work itself, notice what people hold in their hands: the tools they use, their condition, whether they fit the job. Notice the physical environment too, such as the layout, access, noise, and temperature. Watch the sequence and flow: what comes before and after, and where bottlenecks appear.

Questions for this layer might sound like:

- "What are you working on right now?"
- "What makes this part of the job smooth or difficult?"
- "What do you have to work around or tolerate?"

A boilermaker once pointed to the oxy trolley and said, almost casually, "The left wheel on this thing is broken. Getting it across the shop is a mission."

I asked what that meant in practice. He explained that to move it, he often needed another set of hands. But people weren't always free. There were hoses and leads across the floor, materials stacked tight, and just navigating through it took time and patience.

"Sometimes, if the Franna crane is nearby, we lift it with that," he said. "But then you need the crane operator, a spotter, and what could be an easy job becomes a whole production."

I asked how often this happened.

"A few times a week, probably. Depends on what's going on."

"What do you do when you can't get help and the Franna's not available?"

He paused. "You just wrestle the thing yourself. Takes longer. Could drop the whole thing. Not great for your back, but you can't just stop working."

This started at Layer 1 – a broken wheel on a trolley – but staying with it revealed Layer 2 (competing demands on people's time, pressure to keep working), and Layer 3 (the adaptation – solo wrestling of heavy equipment, or a complex workaround involving a crane solution. A single wheel created ripples far beyond itself.

When you understand the work itself, you can start to see what shapes it. What deadlines, demands, or constraints are people responding to? What are they trying to achieve or avoid? That takes you to Layer 2.

Layer 2: The pressures and goals behind it

"FedEx made deadline by thirty seconds. I had FedEx, the other coordinator had StarTrack. Both had half a crew each. It was just a mad, mad rush, push, sweat, scream, just to get the goods out. Severely undermanned ... Only one leading hand on shift every night."

I had asked a freight supervisor what made her work difficult. She described the previous night's shift. There are no procedures that instruct people to sweat, scream, and madly rush. But sometimes, that's what work looks like. Her story revealed the human effort behind the metrics; what it actually takes to hit delivery deadlines when crew sizes don't match the workload.

The freight supervisor's story illustrates why Layer 2 matters. The mad rush, the under-manning, the small margin – none of this appears in procedures. But it shapes every decision made on that shift. Without understanding these pressures, you might see only the visible work (Layer 1) or judge the adaptations (Layer 3) without seeing what drove them.

This is where learning conversations become genuinely useful. They reveal the gap between our assumptions about how work happens (adequate crew, manageable deadlines, orderly execution) and the way things get done (skeleton crews, impossible deadlines, mad rushes). Until leaders understand this gap, improvement efforts will likely miss their mark.

The freight supervisor's story reveals the forces acting on work: time pressure ("thirty seconds to make deadline"), competing goals (speed versus safety), resource constraints ("severely undermanned"). This is where you start to understand why work unfolds the way it does.

Questions that open this layer might sound like:

- "What's important right now?"
- "What are you trying to achieve?"
- "What deadlines or demands shape how you work? What are you trying to avoid – delay, blame, downtime?"

Once you see the pressures people navigate, you can appreciate how they respond. What intelligence do they bring to impossible situations? What adaptations keep things moving? That takes you to Layer 3.

Layer 3: How people adapt

"If I can't find what I need, I go over to Laing O'Rourke and borrow tools from them," one construction worker told me.

Laing O'Rourke was a completely different company on the same site. His colleagues immediately asked him, "What do they get in return?" They knew Laing wasn't running a charity.

After some squirming in the chair, he smiled and said quietly, "There may be a few rolls of shade cloth missing somewhere."

A small black market had emerged, with tools flowing one way and shade cloth flowing the other. Who knows what else! It was a parallel system, off the books, keeping the project moving. A solution out of sight of any procedure, contract, or report.

The black-market story shows Layer 3 in action. The employee didn't just complain about missing tools; he solved the problem through informal coordination. His colleagues understood the parallel economy immediately because they were part of it. It was problematic, yes, but it was also craft. The kind of intelligence that keeps projects moving but never appears in reports.

What you're discovering at this layer is the unofficial system, the workarounds, informal coordination, craft knowledge, and the early warnings that experienced workers notice before anyone else.

Questions that open this layer might sound like:

- "How do you adapt when things don't go to plan?"
- "What tells you something needs attention?"
- "What have you learned that you wish others understood?"

People often feel more vulnerable sharing Layer 3 insights because workarounds can sound like rule-breaking, and adaptations can feel like admitting the system doesn't work. So, this layer often emerges later in a conversation, once trust is established and people sense their intelligence will be appreciated rather than judged.

Understanding these three layers is one thing. Moving through them in actual conversation is another. Learning conversations rarely proceed neatly from Layer 1 to Layer 2 to Layer 3. You might start by asking about the work itself, notice something that hints at pressure, and find yourself in Layer 2. Or someone describes an adaptation (Layer 3), and you realise you need to go back to understand the work better (Layer 1). What matters isn't following a sequence but following the conversation's energy. When something lights up, like a story, a frustration, or a moment of pride, that's your signal to go deeper.

Guiding learning conversations

Once you've started exploring the layers, your main task is to keep the conversation moving towards lived experience and away from abstract opinions. Your role is to help information flow from the work into the conversation, not to signal, prematurely, what you think should happen.

From opinions to examples

Opinions are useful early on because they loosen the room and give people a less risky place to begin. But when you hear opinions stacking on opinions, then it's time to ground the conversation. For example, "This sounds really important. Can you give me an example of how this plays out?" or "Tell me about a time when your supervisor was micro-managing the work."

When people shift to specific examples, scenes, moments, frustrations, and small details, you need to name it. For example, "I'm hearing real examples. Thank you. Good insights usually come from concrete examples like what we just heard." People take their cue from what you highlight, so when you reinforce examples and stories, they lean into that.

In learning conversations, energy and resistance are both information. When someone lights up describing something, that's worth following. When someone deflects or gives a perfunctory answer, that's also worth following, but gently. For example:

- "You said that pretty quickly. Is there more to that story?"

- "You paused just then. What were you thinking about?"

Sometimes, what people don't want to talk about is more revealing than what they do!

The richest insights rarely arrive in the first ten minutes. People need to see that curiosity is real, so they may test you with small, safe stories first. Only once people feel safe do they share the deeper truths – the crafty solution, the quiet conflicts, or the moments of pride or fear.

As the conversation progresses, occasionally reflect back what you're understanding to check alignment and invite correction:

- "So, what I'm hearing is that the time pressure comes from the handover schedule, and that's why you've started ..."

This does several things. First, it shows you're listening carefully. It also gives the person a chance to clarify or add nuance, and finally it helps both of you see the picture forming together. Sometimes people don't realise what they know until they hear you reflect it back.

Ask questions that open rather than close

At a basic level, questions do different kinds of work. Some are designed to verify – they ask for specific information, confirmation, or simple judgement, such as, "What's your job role title?" "Did you follow the procedure?" "Is the permit in place?"

These are closed questions that are useful for establishing facts, confirming understanding, testing knowledge, or keeping a conversation moving. Used occasionally, they help orient the discussion. There is nothing inherently wrong with them, but they tend to narrow attention, pull people towards justification, and signal that the conversation is about checking rather than learning.

Learning conversations rely more heavily on open questions. These invite people to respond in their own words. They don't ask for a data point or a verdict, but for experience, such as:

- "How did you approach it?"
- "What was happening around you at the time?"
- "What influenced the choices you made?"
- "What were you balancing or trading off?"

These questions create space for stories, nuance, and context. They surface the conditions, pressures, and adaptations that shape real work, and instead of testing people, they help the system learn about itself.

The aim is not to eliminate closed questions, but to use them deliberately. In learning conversations, closed questions help you locate yourself, while open questions allow understanding to emerge.

Be careful with "why"

When asking about equipment or process ("Why is that valve here?"), people tend to explain openly. But when "why" lands on behaviour ("Why did you do it that way?"), the conversation often shifts. People become guarded as they feel that have to justify rather than describe.

Try swapping "why" for something gentler, such as:

- "What made that the best option at the time?"
- "How did you decide in that moment?"

You'll receive the same insight without people becoming defensive.

Capturing without disrupting

I once pulled out a notebook mid-conversation and started scribbling. The person stopped mid-sentence and asked, "What are you writing?" The conversation never fully recovered. Now, I wait until I see an opening, such as, "This is really helpful. Would you mind if I jotted down a few notes so I don't forget?"

Learning conversations generate more insight than you can hold in memory. But visible note-taking can make people self-conscious. They start speaking for your notes rather than to you.

Some options:

- Mental notes, written after: Stay fully present during the conversation, jot down key points immediately after. You'll lose some detail but gain authenticity.
- Recording with permission: "Would you mind if I record this? I want to give you my full attention rather than scribbling notes." Most people say yes when framed this way.
- Collaborative noting: In group settings, someone else can capture while you facilitate. Make the notes visible so the group can correct or add.
- Quotes over summaries: Capture people's actual words when possible. Direct quotes carry weight that summaries don't.

Whatever method you choose, tell people what you'll do with what you're learning. If you absolutely need to take notes during the conversations, do so in a way that people can see what you write, you explain why you're doing it, and how you'll use the notes later. Transparency about purpose and use builds trust.

From understanding to action

Learning conversations create understanding, but understanding isn't the endpoint. It's the foundation for better action.

Sometimes learning reveals a problem you can fix immediately, such as a broken tool, a missing resource, or a simple process change. Fix it quickly and tell people you've done so – this shows that conversation leads to action.

More often, learning reveals patterns that require a system-level response, such as competing priorities, design flaws, resource constraints, or misaligned expectations. These can't be fixed in the moment, but they can be carried forward. Your responsibility is ensuring that what you've learned reaches people who can act on it (see *Chapter 10: Building a Conversational Organisation*).

And sometimes, learning simply changes how you see the work. You leave with more respect for the difficulty people navigate, more appreciation for the intelligence they bring, and better questions about what would help. That shift in understanding, in you, is itself valuable. It changes how you lead, how you design, and how you decide.

What learning conversations sound like

You know you're in a real learning conversation when:

- people start speaking from experience instead of abstraction
- you're surprised by what you're hearing
- secrets start to surface, such as the improvised fixes, quiet frustrations, and trade-offs that usually stay hidden
- people begin thinking aloud rather than performing answers
- the hierarchy fades and it stops feeling like you asking them and becomes us figuring it out together

- you leave with better questions than you arrived with
- you feel grateful.

Where to begin

Learning conversations are often the best starting point for conversational practice. They don't require you to challenge, appreciate, or solve anything. They simply ask you to understand.

That simplicity makes them accessible. You can have a learning conversation tomorrow by finding someone doing work you don't fully understand, asking them to walk you through it, following the three layers from surface to depth, noticing what surprises you, and seeing what you learn.

You won't get it perfect, and the first few conversations will feel awkward. You'll miss signals, you'll struggle to know when to move deeper and when to stay at the surface, but that's normal. Conversational capacity grows through practise, not perfection.

What matters is the stance you bring, such as genuine curiosity about how work happens, respect for the people doing it, and willingness to let what you learn change what you thought you knew.

As your confidence grows, you'll notice that the understanding created in these conversations becomes the foundation for other kinds of dialogue. You can't appreciate what works until you understand the work, you can't explore what could be different until you see what is, and you can't invite accountability until you've grasped what people are already navigating.

Learning conversations are how organisations stay in contact with themselves. They're how weak signals travel and how reality speaks when given permission.

The next chapter explores another essential conversation type – appreciative conversations – where we learn not just how work happens, but where it thrives.

CHAPTER 6

Appreciative Conversations

So much of what we do around safety is based on a deficit approach. We point out deviations, shortcomings, incidents, what's missing, or non-compliant. We seem obsessed with a focus on "what's wrong".

Appreciative conversations deliberately lean against that tilt. They shift focus from what erodes value to what creates it. Instead of asking only where things go wrong, they ask where work holds together, where judgement sharpens, and where people act with care and responsibility. The goal is not to disregard weaknesses and what's wrong, but as Peter Drucker said, "to align strengths so that weaknesses become irrelevant".

When I asked leaders at an electricity company in Christchurch, "When did you have your best safety performance?", the answer came immediately, "After the earthquake."

The 2011 quake devastated the city. The grid was down, transformers were unstable, no one could be sure which lines were live, so every job carried real risk. Yet in that period of exhaustion and uncertainty, performance was better than baseline.

People thought for themselves, they coordinated instinctively, and they looked out for one another. The CEO made sandwiches at home and delivered them to field crews because every café was shut.

So, what enabled the crews to work that well during such difficult times?

The conversation uncovered foundations built long before the earthquake. Operators were highly trained and deeply experienced, so trust relationships existed. People knew who to call; whose judgement they could trust. Shared purpose was immediately visible in that the city needed power.

What changed during the crisis wasn't capability but constraint. The bureaucracy that normally slowed decisions disappeared and approval processes fell away. What remained was competence, relationships, and shared purpose. As one supervisor said, "It mattered. Everyone cared about something bigger than themselves, and about each other."

The conversation led to questions about what brought out the best of the people and the organisation, such as:

- What training created that capability? How do we protect it?
- What built those trust relationships before the crisis?
- What bureaucratic constraints disappeared during the earthquake that should stay gone?
- How do we make purpose visible in normal times, not just during crisis?

The safety conversation shifted from "How do we influence people so they make better decisions?" to "How do we create the conditions that allowed excellence during the earthquake recovery?"

Safety conversations aren't just for discovering problems; they're for understanding excellence so it can be protected, strengthened, and spread.

Why appreciation matters for safety

Appreciative conversations focus attention on success – the times when people are alert, coordinated, and acting with care. When judgement sharpens rather than narrows, when people look out for one another, and when work holds together under pressure. These moments reveal the conditions that make safety possible.

This insight sits at the heart of Appreciative Inquiry, developed by David Cooperrider and others. Its central proposition is simple but challenging: organisations move in the direction of what they study. When we study breakdown, we become fluent in breakdown. When we study excellence, we begin to understand how excellence is produced and sustained.

This is true everywhere. We learn how relationships fracture without learning how trust is built, repaired, and sustained. Thriving relationships share patterns worth learning from, such as how people listen, how they recover after strain, how they stay connected when things are difficult. Work is no different.

If we only examine incidents, errors, and non-compliance, we learn how work falls apart, but not how it comes together. Appreciative conversations deliberately broaden the learning lens. They ask: When are we at our best? What conditions allow people to act with care and judgement? Which supports, relationships, and rhythms make good work more likely?

When leaders take time to notice and name what is working, several important shifts occur:

Confidence is restored. People recognise that their everyday professionalism already contributes to safety. That confidence supports ownership rather than compliance.

Trust deepens. Naming what works signals belief in people's competence and intent. When people feel trusted, they're far more willing to share what is fragile, unfinished, or difficult.

Space for honesty opens. Appreciation lowers defensiveness and creates room for honest reflection. Conversations about risk, error, or change are more likely to be met with curiosity than judgement.

Conditions for excellence become visible. By studying moments of success, we bring to the surface the social, technical, and psychological conditions that allow performance to thrive. This gives the organisation something concrete to protect, strengthen, and replicate.

Appreciation doesn't replace learning from failure – it completes it.

A framework for appreciation

When you enter an appreciative conversation, you're not just collecting compliments or boosting morale. You're investigating success with the same rigour that most organisations reserve for investigating failure.

But what exactly are you appreciating? Three levels help focus your attention:

Level 1: Individual capability

The skills, judgement, expertise, and care that people bring to their work. What someone does well, how they think, what they notice, and how they respond.

Level 2: Relational coordination
How people work together. The patterns of communication, mutual support, and shared attention that allow teams to function well. The informal systems that hold work together.

Level 3: System conditions
What the organisation provides that makes good work possible, such as resources, relationships, time, tools, trust, and clarity. The structures and rhythms that support rather than hinder.

These levels nest inside each other. Individual capability flourishes when coordination works well. Coordination thrives when system conditions support it. And system conditions only become visible when you start by appreciating what individuals and teams do well.

Think of these as moving from the visible to the invisible, from what one person does to what the whole system makes possible.

Level 1: Individual capability

Start with what you can see. Ask, What does this person do well? How do they think? What do they notice that others miss?

"Who around here do you look up to for the way they work?" I asked Steve, a mining truck driver during a site visit.

He thought for a moment. "Sarah."

"What is it that Sarah does that you find impressive?"

He paused, searching for the words. "Well, it's like she's always ready to jump in when something's needed."

"Tell me more. What does she do that shows she's ready to jump in?"

Another pause. "It's almost like she knows what's going to happen next. She understands what's happening, what different needs are around the site. She's a truck operator like me, but she's always switched on."

"Switched on how?"

"She's got the bigger picture of what's happening on site. She knows where her work fits in. She sees the missing piece of the puzzle. Doesn't call it in before it's needed, but when someone does need help, she's already good to go."

I could hear the respect in his voice.

"You've clearly observed what makes Sarah good at this. Have you told her?"

"No," he said, surprised by the question. "Why would I?"

"Because what you've just described – how she reads the whole operation, her readiness to help out – that's expertise worth recognising. Does management know what makes her valuable?"

"Probably not. They just see that she's reliable."

"But you see more than that. You see how she's reliable, the intelligence behind it, and you've noticed that she understands the bigger picture, that she positions herself to help, anticipates what's needed. That's systems thinking."

Steven nodded slowly. "Yeah, I guess I do see that."

What started as a question about who he looked up to had become something else. Steve had articulated expertise that was largely invisible. He'd named capabilities that no job description captures, that no training program teaches, and that no performance metric measures. This is systems thinking. Anticipatory positioning. Reading operational rhythm.

And by helping him see that he was seeing this, the organisation gains an understanding of what capability looks like in this work. Not just technical skill, or operating the equipment safely, but the operational intelligence that makes the whole system flow smoothly. This is capability worth developing in new drivers, worth protecting when restructures happen, and worth recognising when performance is assessed.

This is what Level 1 appreciation does. Sometimes it helps people recognise capability in others, and in that recognition, they often discover they're developing it themselves. Or at a minimum, they're making visible what excellence looks like, which helps the whole organisation learn what to nurture and protect.

Questions that open up this level:

- "When does this work feel like it's going really well?"
- "What are you particularly good at in this job?"
- "What do you notice that helps you stay ahead of problems?"
- "Tell me about a time when your judgement really mattered."
- "What have you learned over the years that makes you effective?"
- "What would someone new struggle with that you handle easily now?"
- "Who around here do you look up to for the way they work?"

When people deflect

Most people deflect when asked what they are doing well in their work – "I'm just doing my job." "Anyone would do the same." This isn't necessarily false modesty as competence often becomes invisible to us. So, slow it down. "You say, 'just doing my job', but can you walk me through what that actually involves?" Or, "What tells you when something's not quite right?"

The goal is helping people articulate knowledge that's become tacit. When they start describing their judgement, cues, and techniques, they're not just answering your questions. They're discovering what they know.

Once you understand what someone does well, you can start to see what makes it possible. What relationships support this work? What informal coordination happens? That takes you to Level 2.

In Steve's story, the hint is already there; he learned by paying attention to how Sarah operated. That is informal mentoring, or peer observation; a culture where excellence is visible enough to be modelled. These are relational patterns that enable capability to develop and spread.

Level 2: Relational coordination

Level 2 shows you the social fabric of work. These are the informal systems of communication, mutual support, and shared attention that make collective performance possible. It's how people coordinate without formal meetings, how they read each other, cover for each other, and share knowledge. The unspoken agreements that make cooperation smooth.

This is often the most invisible layer. People don't usually think about how they work together, they just do it, but this coordination is where much of safety lives.

What to notice

Pay attention to:

- Informal communication: How information travels between people.
- Mutual awareness: How people track what others are doing.
- Shared responsibility: How people look out for each other.
- Knowledge sharing: How expertise spreads through a team.
- Trust patterns: Who people turn to, who they rely on.
- Recovery and repair: How people handle mistakes or strain.

Questions that open up this level:

- "How does the team coordinate when things get busy?"
- "Who do you turn to when you need help?"
- "How do you know what your colleagues are doing without asking?"
- "What makes this team work well together?"
- "When was a time that the team really pulled together?"
- "What would fall apart if the relationships here changed?"

From "we work well together" to understanding how

When people say, "We work well together," that's the beginning, not the end of inquiry. Deepen it by asking:

- "What does 'working well together' actually look like? Give me an example."
- "How do you know when someone needs help before they ask?"
- "What's something you do for each other that isn't in any procedure?"

The goal is making the invisible visible. Surfacing the coordination patterns that hold work together.

The deviant manual-handling training

In 2017, a catering company asked me to visit one of their outlier sites. The numbers told a clear story of better incident stats, higher retention, and stronger engagement scores than any sister site. The company wanted to understand why. Some suspected the numbers were fudged, while others thought the site might genuinely be doing something worth learning from.

I arrived expecting to find a charismatic leader or some innovative safety program. What I found was something less glamorous. In a commercial kitchen were two chefs. When asked to rate the site from one to ten, they looked at each other and agreed, "Seven, maybe eight."

"Has it always been a seven or eight?" I asked.

"No, no, no," they said, almost in unison. One of them leaned forward. "Two, three years ago? This place was a three. Maybe worse."

That shift, from three to eight, was the opening. "What changed?"

They glanced at each other again, and then said something I didn't expect: "The manual-handling training."

I'd heard about manual-handling training at other sites. It was usually dismissed as useless, even insulting, with comments like, "You can't lift the way they teach you in those videos!" But here, something had been different.

"What made it so good?" I asked.

"The lady who ran it didn't just show us the videos and leave," one chef said. "She came into the kitchen afterwards. She wanted to see what we actually had to lift."

"And we showed her," the other added. "The big pots. The heavy bags high up on the shelves. The stuff that's in the freezer with the slippery floor."

"What happened?"

"She watched us work. Quickly, she could see that, half the time, you can't do it the way they teach in the training. Loads are too heavy. Spaces are too tight. Things are too high up. Sometimes there's just no good way to lift something."

There was a pause. I waited.

"So, someone asked her, 'What do we do then?'"

The chef smiled slightly, remembering. "She thought about it for a moment. Then she said, 'That's when you ask for help.'"

It was such a simple phrase, but the way they said it, I could tell it had landed differently than most safety advice.

"Before that," one of them explained, "asking for help felt like admitting you couldn't do your job. Like you were weak or slow. So, people just struggled through, or they'd do something dodgy to manage alone."

"And now?"

"Now it's just what you do. If something's too heavy or awkward, you say, 'Can you give me a hand?' and someone comes over. No one thinks twice about it."

"How did that spread?" I asked. "The facilitator left after the training, right?"

"Yeah, but it stuck. I think because she framed it as professional, not weak. Like, the smart thing is knowing when you need help. And once a few people started doing it, it became normal."

I noticed they kept saying "we" and "someone". "Who helps when you ask?"

"Anyone nearby. Whoever's free. We just sort of keep track of what everyone's doing."

"How do you keep track?"

They looked at each other, slightly puzzled by the question. "You just ... know. You hear the oven timer; you know someone's going to be pulling trays. You see someone heading to the freezer room, you know they might need a hand with stock."

"So, you're paying attention to each other."

"I guess so. Yeah, we are."

What started as a story about manual-handling training was a story about how a team learned to coordinate. Asking for help became a shared practice. Helping each other became the rhythm of the work. And paying attention to what colleagues needed became part of how they stayed safe.

The training didn't teach them to lift differently. It taught them to work together differently.

Moving deeper

Once you see how people coordinate, you can start to ask what makes that coordination possible. What did the organisation provide? What conditions supported this way of working? That takes you to Level 3.

In the kitchen story, the facilitator's willingness to come into the workspace – to see the real constraints and stay long enough to offer honest guidance – were system conditions. Time was provided and trust was extended. The training wasn't rushed through as a compliance exercise. That organisational choice made the relational shift possible.

Level 3: System conditions

The deepest level of appreciation reveals what the organisation provides that makes good work possible. Not what individuals overcome despite the system, but what the system actively enables.

This is where appreciative inquiry becomes organisational learning. You discover what's worth protecting, replicating, and strengthening across the system.

What to notice

Pay attention to:

- Resources and tools: What the organisation provides that actually helps.

- Time and rhythm: Schedules, cycles, and pace that support good work.
- Relationships and access: Who people can reach, and how easily.
- Clarity and alignment: Shared understanding of purpose and priorities.
- Trust and autonomy: Space for judgement, permission to adapt.
- Learning infrastructure: How knowledge spreads, how improvement happens.

Questions that open up this level:

- "What does the organisation provide that makes your work easier?"
- "What would you lose if you moved to another site or company?"
- "What conditions here allow you to work the way you do?"
- "What's different about this place compared to others you've worked at?"
- "If you were designing the ideal setup, what from here would you keep?"
- "What are we getting right that we should protect?"

From individual excellence to system insight

The power of moving through all three levels is that individual excellence becomes a lens for seeing system conditions.

When someone describes their expertise (Level 1), and you help them see how they coordinate with others (Level 2), you can then ask, "What makes all this possible?"

Often, they'll say, "Well, we have time to talk to each other." Or, "The supervisor trusts us to figure it out." Or, "We've been together long enough to know each other's style."

These are system conditions – time, trust, stability, relationships – and they're often fragile. The organisation might not realise it's providing them, or they might be about to change something that disrupts them.

When the runway keeps working

At an airport in New Zealand, runway resurfacing work happens throughout the year. The work happens at night, between the last landing and the first departure. It's highly collaborative, time-critical, and unforgiving. A shift can't end with a hole in the tarmac. If something goes wrong, planes don't fly.

Year after year, the work runs smoothly. There's no heroics, no drama, and if the team has done their job well, nobody notices they were even there.

My colleague Rob spent time with James, a general manager at the airport, trying to understand why this maintenance program worked so well.

"What makes this different?" he asked.

James thought for a moment. "It's the partnership structure. We're not hiring contractors project-by-project. This is a twenty-year plan. Same partners, year after year."

"What does that long-term structure give you?"

"Relationships," he said. "Real ones. You can't build trust in a three-month contract. People are guarded. They're worried about what they're getting versus what they're delivering. But over years? There's give and take. You develop good working relationships."

Level 1 starting to appear: Individual capability

Rob asked about the night works. How did they handle the pressure, the tight timelines?

"The crews are experienced," James said. "They know the work. But more than that, they know each other. During one shift, two workers noticed their foreman hadn't had enough sleep. They sent him home. They were recognised for speaking up."

"That takes confidence."

"It does. But it's not just individual confidence, it's the whole setup."

Level 2: Relational coordination becoming visible

"Tell me about the setup."

"Well, we specify in our bids that we expect open, collaborative communication. We meet people before putting them on contracts. We're explicit about culture. We grow a culture where we reward and recognise each other, where we're open and honest with each other and actually have a laugh."

"That sounds deliberate."

"It is. We pay what's fair and reasonable and don't try to pay less than that. We've had numerous difficult, contentious conversations. We put our pride at the door. We're here for the project."

Level 3: System conditions emerging

"What else makes this possible?"

James described the governance structure. Nine people meeting quarterly, not to police performance but to ask, "Do the teams have the tools, capacity, and capability they need? What support can we provide?"

He described the innovation KPI, where three innovations per year are expected and supported, such as trying new paving mixes, testing different products, or finding ways to work smarter, quicker, safer.

He described how partners were selected not just for technical capability but for willingness to work openly, to argue well, to stay in the room when conversations get uncomfortable.

"What would have to change for this to stop working?" my colleague asked.

"Personnel change," James said immediately. "If we brought in someone who didn't support the working alliance or share the values. The partnership is bigger than one person. We review succession planning annually because we know the culture needs to be embedded in the company, not just held by individuals."

"And have you come close to that?"

"Once," he said. "We had someone join who kept pushing for cheaper contractors. They were always asking, 'Why are we paying this much?' It created tension. The kind that breaks trust. We had to have some hard conversations about what we were actually building here."

"What happened?"

"They came around, but it showed how fragile this is. One person with the wrong mindset can unravel years of work."

Recognition of fragility: System conditions can be lost

As the conversation continued, the system conditions became clearer:

- Stability and continuity: Twenty-year contracts instead of short-term projects. Same partners, building relationships over time.
- Aligned incentives: Fair payment, not cheapest price. Shared risk and value.
- Governance focus: Supporting teams, not policing them. Quarterly meetings asking, "What do you need?" not "Why didn't you deliver?"

- Cultural investment: Recognition systems, speaking up rewarded, wellbeing prioritised (Saturday night work rejected because "we don't want to burn people out").
- Selection for values: Choosing partners who can have difficult conversations, who put pride aside, who stay in the room.
- Innovation as expectation: Annual KPI requiring experimentation, not just compliance.
- Time for relationships: Daily contact between partners. Workshops bringing thirty-plus people together to plan collaboratively.

These were designed features. The airport had learned from experience and deliberately created conditions that made excellent work more likely. And the result was a runway that quietly keeps working, where crews feel confident raising concerns, where supervisors trust their people's judgement. Partners challenged each other constructively, so that work got done well, year after year.

Level 3 appreciation reveals the system conditions that make excellence possible, often before the organisation realises it could lose them. When my colleague asked what the work program had taught the airport, James said, "It's provided a process, a culture, and a team that's held in high regard for people on other projects to aspire to."

The airport hadn't just created a successful maintenance program. They'd created a template for how work could be done differently. And by taking time to appreciate what made it work, not just the individual skills or team coordination, but the system conditions enabling both, they could protect it, replicate it, and help it spread.

Appreciative patterns

You know appreciation is happening when people move from describing tasks to expressing meaning. "I wanted to make sure she got home safe," instead of "I gave her a ride." People slow down and savour the memory of having been part of something good. They give credit away. The role of expertise becomes more visible among the systems, goals, and procedures guiding work. Vulnerability appears and people become willing to talk about what's hard alongside what's working.

Individual appreciative conversations create local insight, but their real power emerges when patterns become visible across many conversations.

When you hear the same capability named repeatedly across different people, you're seeing a strength worth protecting. When the same system condition appears in multiple stories, you've found something the organisation is getting right. When the same relational pattern shows up in high-performing teams, you've discovered something worth replicating.

This is where appreciative conversations connect to Chapter 10's work on movement-making. The stories you collect in appreciative conversations become the stories that travel. They reveal:

- what capabilities exist that the organisation might not know about
- what coordination patterns work that aren't in any procedure
- what system conditions support excellence that might be fragile
- what's worth protecting during times of change
- what should be replicated rather than reinvented.

Your role is helping these insights travel to where they can inform decisions about:

- Resource allocation: Protect what enables good work.
- System design: Replicate conditions that support excellence.
- Change management: Don't accidentally destroy what's working.
- Hiring and development: Look for and grow the capabilities that matter.
- Recognition and reward: Value what actually creates safety.

Why this matters

Appreciative conversations don't replace learning from failure, they don't eliminate the need for investigation, correction, or accountability, and they don't pretend that problems don't exist or that risk isn't real. What they do is identify where strengths can be boosted, to make weaknesses more irrelevant.

When organisations only study failure they become fluent in breakdown but ignorant of what holds work together. They know a thousand ways things can go wrong, but they can't articulate what makes them go right. They pile on controls without understanding what already works. They change things without knowing what they're disrupting.

Appreciative conversations give organisations a way to learn from their own success, to understand the capabilities they've developed, the coordination they've achieved, and the conditions they've created. This enables them to see what's worth protecting before it's lost, and they can replicate patterns that work rather than repeatedly solving the same problems.

The work of safety is not just preventing harm. It's also recognising and nurturing what allows people to work well. And appreciative conversations make both possible.

The next chapter explores possibility conversations: how to help people imagine what could be different and turn local ingenuity into organisational learning.

CHAPTER 7

Possibility Conversations

At a mining workshop, a mechanic showed me how to bypass a safety control. It was unsettling, surprising, and also understandable.

The official procedure had become cumbersome and unreasonable as the work required him to climb up and down a seven-metre ladder twenty times during fault-finding. His, and the team's, workaround cut that to one. It was faster, less exhausting, and arguably as safe, but it was also unofficial, hidden, and technically non-compliant.

That moment sits at the heart of possibility conversations. People are already innovating; they're finding better ways to work. The question is, "Does the organisation have conversations where those innovations can surface, be examined, and evolve into something the whole system can learn from?"

Possibility conversations help people move from coping with constraints to imagining beyond them. They create space between "this is how we make it work" and "this is how it could work better". They turn workarounds into prototypes, frustration into design questions, and local ingenuity into organisational learning.

This chapter shows you how to open those conversations, how to help ideas move from private to shared, and how to turn possibility into change.

The isolation lock workaround

"Can I see how you do that?" I asked a truck mechanic at a mining workshop. He was cleaning a fuel pump that would go back into one of the massive haul trucks.

"Sure, come with me."

We walked together towards the truck. Before stepping under its massive frame, he instructed me to place my isolation lock on the lock panel – a control to prevent anyone from starting the truck while someone is working in the danger zone.

"Nice," I said. "I'm always given these locks during site visits, but I've never actually used one. Can you show me what to do?"

As he demonstrated the process, I brought up a recent incident on another site. Someone had broken open an isolation lock after the person who owned it left the workshop and wasn't available to remove it when colleagues needed to start the truck.

"I don't see how anyone could break this lock open," I said.

"Oh, that's easy," he said, pulling a screwdriver from his pocket. With a few quick movements, he showed me how the plates could be bent apart to free the panel. It took maybe ten seconds.

It was a clear violation of one of the company's life-saving rules. In that moment, I had a choice. I could respond with alarm, correction, and discipline, or I could stay curious about why he knew this.

"In your experience, when do these locks become frustrating to use?"

He thought for a moment. "When you're fault-finding," he said. "To get to the driver's cabin and start the truck, you have to climb seven metres up. If it doesn't work, you climb back down, put yours and everyone else's locks back on, make a small change, then take them all off again and climb up. You might have to do that twenty times. It takes forever. It's incredibly frustrating."

"What other solutions have you seen that make this easier to work with?"

"Well," he said, his voice dropping slightly, "we've come up with something. One person stays in the cab while the rest of us do visual verification and give an okay signal when it's safe to remove or apply the lock. So effectively we put their lock on and off. It saves a lot of time."

We discussed the risks and benefits of this adaptation. What made it safer than the official method in some ways, and what risks it introduced, as well as what they'd learned about making it work.

"That's actually pretty clever," I said. "You've solved a real problem. What would it take to make that solution safe and official?"

He looked surprised. "You think that's possible?"

"I don't know, but it sounds worth exploring."

Later, back in the head office, I shared the story with management. There was shock and upset but also intrigue. A quiet "why not?" The conversation began to travel, shaping shared assumptions about what was acceptable and what might be possible. Through several discussions and reviews, the company developed a new, approved procedure that incorporated the principle of the workaround, safely.

It was a small example of safety evolving with the work.

From workaround to innovation

To turn insight into innovation, we often have to resist our reflex for quick fixes. When we move too quickly from observation to solution, we risk solving the wrong problem, adding friction rather than removing it.

The isolation lock story shows this pattern. Rather than simply enforcing the isolation lock use or reacting to the violation, the conversation explored when and why the system became frustrating. That understanding led to a solution that preserved safety while reducing friction.

As design thinkers often say, "Fall in love with the problem, not the solution." That means understanding what a workaround is protecting, saving, or making possible before deciding what should replace it. When you understand the need deeply, the solution often suggests itself, but when you jump to solutions, you risk solving the wrong problem.

Several forces push us towards quick fixes:

- Jumping to solutions feels productive. Saying "we'll buy new equipment" or "we'll add a procedure" gives the impression of decisive action. Understanding why something frustrates people feels slower, mushier, less concrete.
- Leaders want to be seen as problem-solvers. The fix-it reflex is strong. When someone brings you a problem, the instinct is to solve it immediately, not to spend time understanding it.
- Understanding takes patience. You must sit with discomfort and listen to frustration. Follow threads that don't lead anywhere obvious. It requires tolerance for ambiguity that most organisations struggle with.
- Workarounds look like non-compliance. When you see someone bypassing a control, the trained response is correction,

not curiosity. It takes deliberate effort to ask, "Why are they doing this?" instead of, "How do we make them stop?"

When you encounter a workaround or a solution that is wanting, try this sequence:

Resist the urge to fix. Your first instinct will be to fix, stop, or redirect. Pause. There's intelligence here worth understanding first.

Surface the need. Ask what the workaround achieves. What problem does it solve? What would happen if they stopped doing it?

Understand what would be lost. If you "fixed" this workaround by enforcing the official method, what would people lose? Efficiency? Safety? Sanity? Understanding the cost helps you design better responses.

Test your understanding. "So, the real issue is that the official method creates twenty frustrating climbs, and you've found a way to reduce that to one while maintaining safety. Is that right?" Check whether you've grasped the need accurately.

Explore options together. "What would make this solution even better? What risks concern you? What would need to change to make this official?"

When I brought the isolation lock story back to management, the first response was, "They're violating the procedure. We need to stop it."

"Before we do that," I said, "what if we understood what they're trying to achieve?"

Instead of enforcement, we started talking about efficiency. And instead of compliance, we talked about reducing unnecessary burden. This shifted the conversation from the workaround to instead be about the solution to a problem we hadn't designed for.

When we do this well, system responses are more likely to support judgement, ownership, and care rather than crowd them out. The approved procedure that emerged from the isolation lock conversation did both; it maintained the control while acknowledging the intelligence in how people had adapted.

Nathan's rebars story

Nathan was doing his monthly "day-in-the-shoes" experience, spending a shift with a civil crew. At one point, he noticed something interesting. The crew was bending rebar so that the ends pointed towards the ground, reducing the stabbing hazard if someone fell. The rebars were of different diameters, up to 22mm. The team used a piece of cut-off scaffolding pipe, sliding it onto the bar to create a clear bending point and a more ergonomic way to apply force.

Nathan was intrigued. "Why are you using this tool?"

"We have nothing else," came the reply.

"But is this allowed?"

"No, there's no procedure for it."

The method wasn't approved, but it worked. Taking it away would leave the team with no safe alternative. Nathan could have noted the deviation and moved on. Instead, he stayed curious. He asked how long they'd been doing it this way, what other methods they'd tried, and why this worked better.

The conversation shifted. He recognised the ingenuity in what the crew had developed. They hadn't been careless or cutting corners, they'd solved a real problem in the absence of proper equipment. That appreciation opened space for something else.

"What if we made this official?" Nathan asked.

He called the scaffolding manufacturer for the tube's specifications, consulted engineers to assess load capacities, and eventually helped develop an approved, purpose-built tool.

Opening possibility

Possibility conversations require different conditions than learning or appreciative conversations. People need permission to critique the current state and imagine alternatives. They need to feel that their ideas matter, that speaking up won't backfire, and that possibility is real, not performative.

"I know the system makes this hard. I'm not suggesting you're doing anything wrong. I'm just curious about what would make it better." Then ask questions that open space, such as, "If you could redesign this from scratch, what would you keep and what would you change?" Or, "What's one small change that would remove a big frustration?"

Permission grows when you respond to first ideas with genuine interest. Even one idea dismissed or explained away kills the conversation. Treat early ideas as drafts, not final proposals. Your job is to help them develop, not to evaluate them.

Avoid questions that close things down. "Any suggestions?" is too vague. "Why don't you just ..." sounds like you already know the answer.

You'll hit predictable resistance – "That'll never work here." "We've tried that before." When this happens, acknowledge their reality. "I hear that it feels impossible. What would need to change to make it possible?"

Sometimes ideas are too abstract, such as, "We need better communication." Ground them by saying, for example, "What would better communication look like in practice? Give me an example."

People will minimise their own ideas ... "It's probably dumb, but ..." So, reframe it: "You called it a workaround. I'd call it innovation. Walk me through it."

You'll know possibility is opening up when the conversation changes texture. Where there's spaciousness rather than urgency, then people lean forward, they start building on each other's ideas. Someone says, "What if we ..." or "Actually, that reminds me ..." The energy will start to rise. Uncertainty is present, but it feels creative rather than anxious.

The goal isn't to generate perfect solutions. It's to create space where ideas that have been sitting privately can become shared, where workarounds can be examined for their intelligence, and where people can think together about what might be different.

The workshop improvement team

At a mine site workshop, I asked a group of fitters for their ideas for making the place better. They weren't shy, but they didn't ask for anything grand or unrealistic. Most of what frustrated them could be improved without anyone's permission.

> It's not permission to break rules, but permission to imagine better ones.

The parts store was disorganised, so finding what you needed took longer than it should. The layout had grown organically over the years, but nobody had stepped back to think about whether it still worked.

The dressing room was on the opposite side of the facility from the workshop. Every day, people walked a couple of minutes each way just to change, occasionally yielding to the forklift that also operated in that area. It was a small inefficiency, but it added up.

Scrap metal was piled up in corners. It wasn't dangerous, but it cluttered the space and represented wasted value.

The team chose three ideas to start with and began that week:

- They reorganised the parts store with a clearer layout and labelling.
- They moved the dressing room closer to the workshop, cutting minutes off everyone's day.
- They sorted and sold the scrap metal, clearing space and generating revenue.

It was nothing dramatic, but simple things that made work easier.

What struck me was watching what happened next. The workshop began to feel different. People moved with less friction, small frustrations disappeared, and because the team had agency to fix what annoyed them, they kept looking for more improvements. It felt good and meaningful to them to make their workplace better.

Over the following years, that workshop consistently recorded the highest engagement scores across the company. Because people had been trusted to shape their own work environment, possibility had become part of how the place operated.

This pattern appears in high-performing organisations everywhere. Toyota's quality circles work the same way: small groups of people who know the work best come together regularly, name what could be improved, and act on the ideas within reach. This results in countless small changes over time – nothing fancy, just what organisations do when they're serious about giving people agency to improve their own work.

When possibility needs authority

Not every good idea can be acted on locally. Some require resources, approval, or system-level change. When possibility conversations bring to the surface ideas that exceed local authority, leaders have two responsibilities:

Carry the idea upward. Translate what you've heard to people who can act on it. Not as "The workers think we should ..." but as, "Here's what we learned about how work actually happens, and here's what it's pointing towards."

The isolation lock story travelled from workshop to head office because I carried it. I didn't just report the violation, I explained the need, showed the intelligence in the workaround, and framed it as an opportunity rather than a problem.

Stay close to the people with the idea. While the system responds, or doesn't, people need to know their idea was heard and taken seriously. Even if the answer is "not now", explain why. Ideas die in silence.

When people see ideas travel and receive real consideration, even if they're not all implemented, possibility stays alive. When ideas disappear into the system and nothing comes back, cynicism grows faster than if you'd never asked.

Why possibility matters

Most organisations have more good ideas than they realise. They're just not having conversations where those ideas can surface, be tested, and taken seriously.

Every day, people encounter friction points, whether it's tasks that don't quite fit, procedures that almost work, tools that need refinement, or controls that create more risk than they reduce. Each moment contains the seed of improvement, but most systems don't know how to listen to those seeds or help them grow.

Possibility conversations change that. They treat workarounds as prototypes, not problems. They frame frustration as design intelligence, help frontline ingenuity inform system design, and create space between coping with constraints and changing them.

When organisations practise possibility regularly, safety stops being something done to people and becomes something built with them. People shift from "I have to work around this" to "We could change this." From resignation to agency – from compliance to co-creation.

The isolation lock that started this chapter began as a violation. It ended as an innovation. That transformation happened because someone was willing to stay curious instead of corrective, to explore the intelligence in the workaround before shutting it down, and to ask, "What if we made this better instead of just insisting it's wrong?"

That's what possibility conversations create. It's not permission to break rules, but permission to imagine better ones. It's not fantasy divorced from constraints, but grounded creativity that takes reality seriously while refusing to accept it as fixed.

The next chapter explores how possibility becomes commitment, and how conversations shift from "What could be different?" to "What will we do about it?"

CHAPTER 8

Accountability Conversations

Hugh Goddard, a managing director of a construction business, was walking a project site in Auckland when he noticed a team member without a hard hat. There was no immediate risk of falling objects, but the rule was clear.

Most safety leaders know what usually comes next: a reprimand, a reminder of policy, perhaps a note in a system. Predictable and procedural, it may nudge behaviour, but it rarely changes anything deeper. But that is not what Hugh did.

He walked over and said, quietly, “It’s up to you whether you wear your hard hat or not. It’s your head, yours to protect. But if we don’t look after these basics, we won’t be trusted with more work from the client.”

The employee looked up, surprised. There was no threat, no policing, no demand to comply. Hugh had reframed the moment. Wearing the hard hat was no longer about obeying a rule. It was about care for the team, the company, and the future they were trying to build together.

The worker wasn't forced but invited to choose.

That is at the heart of accountability conversations. They connect expectations to meaning and strengthen commitment by appealing to what people already care about. Paul Stepczak captured this dynamic perfectly when he said, "If people can't see themselves in the outcome, they won't show up for the process." This is what Hugh understood intuitively. He didn't demand compliance with a rule; he helped the team member see himself in the outcome.

Why broadcasting rules isn't enough

Most organisations are good at broadcasting expectations by telling people what to do through procedures, policies, toolbox talks, and campaigns. They're good at checking compliance through audits, observations, and inspections. And they're good at correcting deviations through discipline, retraining, and consequences.

Then the cycle is repeated.

This approach creates temporary behaviour change, at best. People comply when they're being watched, and they perform safety when someone with authority is present. But the moment supervision fades, behaviour is likely to drift back.

The problem isn't that people don't care about safety, but that the expectation never became personally meaningful. It remained external. An accountability was imposed on them rather than something they chose for themselves.

Accountability conversations do something different. Instead of broadcasting expectations and checking compliance, they help people see themselves in the expectation. They connect what's being asked to what people already value, care about, and want to protect.

When that connection forms, compliance transforms into commitment. People follow through not because they're being watched, but because they recognise themselves in what's being asked.

The questions become, "What makes expectations personally meaningful?" "What are the sources of genuine commitment?"

Six currents of accountability

When expectations stick, and when they land as genuine commitment rather than mere compliance, it's because they've connected to something people already care about. Not in one formulaic way, but through several overlapping currents or dimensions.

These are aspects to notice and draw on. Sometimes one dominates, other times several appear together. What matters is recognising which currents are present in this conversation, with this person, in this moment.

Seeing your impact

The work matters because someone else depends on it.

"Tell me about a time when you did something for someone else here on site."

The group of vehicle operators looked a bit surprised by my question, but one of them started. "I always bring cleaning spray and cloths to my truck. Mostly because I hate sitting in a dirty cab all day. So, whenever there's a bit of downtime, I dust, wipe, polish the driver's cabin and so on. Sure, it's for myself, but when I leave at the end of the day, I know that whoever drives that truck next will arrive in a clean work environment."

His colleagues nodded. Someone added, "The opposite is so true. I hate getting into a truck and finding a used pair of ear plugs on the seat. It's disgusting."

What started as self-interest had become care for others. The operator wasn't following a procedure about truck cleanliness. He was thinking about the person who came after him; making their day a little better. Showing respect through small acts.

Abstract expectations become concrete responsibilities when people can see who benefits from their work or who suffers when it fails. It's no longer about following a procedure, it's about protecting a colleague, making someone's day easier, or preventing someone from inheriting your mess.

Questions that bring this to the surface:

- "Who's affected when this goes well? When it goes poorly?"
- "What happens to the next person if this step is skipped?"
- "Tell me about a time when someone else's careful work made your day easier."

The bigger picture

The work matters because it contributes to an outcome people value.

When I asked an electrical asset inspector how he saw his job, he laughed and said, "My supervisor told me I'd won the lottery when I got this role. Back then I thought he meant the job security."

At first, he saw himself as the person who checked poles and filled in forms. Drive, park, walk the line, record the condition, move on. Important, yes, but small. A long way from the drama of storm response or big construction jobs. "I figured the real work was what the lineys did," he said. "We just ticked boxes, so they knew where to go."

Then someone showed him the numbers: forty to fifty per cent of all fieldwork was triggered by asset inspections. Miss something, and it becomes an emergency breakdown. Catch it early, and it becomes planned work with better control over risk and cost.

"We're the only ones who systematically assess the quality of the network," he told me. "Without us it'd just be fixing breakdowns or guessing."

That landed for him in a practical way. He started to see each inspection as a decision point that could remove risk from someone else's day months or years later. A rushed assessment might mean a crew climbing a structure in bad weather to deal with an avoidable fault. A thorough one could turn the same issue into a routine job on a calm Tuesday.

Recently he'd been spending more time out with the line crews as a spotter, certified for pole rescue. "I see the jobs that came out of my inspections," he said. "I see the conditions they're working in. It makes me even more determined to get my bit right. If I do this well, I'm making their work safer and easier before they even get there."

He hadn't changed roles. The tasks were still the same: walk, look, record. But his sense of accountability had shifted. He no longer saw himself as someone who "just" inspected assets. He saw himself as part of the system that keeps people off faulty structures, prevents breakdowns, and protects the communities those lines serve.

When people understand how their part fits into the whole system, their work gains significance beyond the task itself. They're not just completing a step. They're contributing to something larger that they can take pride in.

This is particularly powerful for people in roles that feel removed from the final outcome. When someone in planning, procurement, administration, or inspection can see the direct line between their work and what happens in the field, their decisions carry different weight.

Questions that bring this to the surface include:

- "How does your work connect to what happens before and after?"
- "What breaks down elsewhere if this step isn't done well?"
- "What becomes possible when this is done well?"

Trusted to think, not just follow

The work matters because your judgement is valued, not just your compliance.

One electricity company developed twelve approved methods for live-line work. Each met the same standard but allowed line workers to choose the method that best suited the conditions. It didn't create chaos; it created ownership. As one supervisor said, "The guys loved it. They felt trusted to think again."

When organisations remove unnecessary constraints and trust people to navigate the work intelligently, accountability lands because people are trusted to exercise it.

I've worked with organisations where every tiny variation from procedure required permission. Workers learned to stop thinking and just follow instructions. When things went wrong, they could point to the procedure they followed. Responsibility had been removed along with autonomy.

I've also worked with organisations where people were given clear boundaries and were trusted to think within them. Standards were high, but people had room to adapt to conditions, to use their judgement, to solve problems. The accountability in those places was deeper because people felt responsible, not just obedient.

Questions that bring this to the surface include:

- "Where do you feel trusted to make decisions?"
- "What gets in the way of using your judgement?"
- "When do you feel like a professional versus when do you feel micromanaged?"

Becoming good at something

The work matters because developing skill is inherently satisfying.

When I trained as a commercial pilot, there was a lot to comply with, from checklists and flight paths to standardised radio calls. But I never thought of those things as "compliance". To me, they were craft, requiring precision and discipline. Things to get good at.

Following the checklist wasn't about avoiding punishment. It was about being professional and doing something difficult well. It was about the quiet satisfaction that comes from executing a challenging task with competence.

Mastery doesn't replace safety standards; it transforms how people relate to them. When standards connect to craft and expertise, people want to meet them because excellence matters to them.

I've seen this in maintenance crews who take pride in their diagnostic skills, in operators who compete to achieve the smoothest handovers, and in safety advisors who develop genuine expertise in understanding how work happens. When people can see themselves getting better at something worth doing well, standards become part of that pursuit rather than obstacles to it.

Questions that bring this to the surface include:

- "What took you the longest to learn here?"
- "What's a skill you're proud of?"
- "What would make you really good at this job versus just adequate?"

Protecting people you care about

The work matters because people matter to you.

I once attended a prestart meeting at a maintenance facility in Brisbane. The safety person was standing in front of the group going through the latest broadcast about what's important and asking people to look out for each other. As I looked around the room, people seemed disengaged – they were leaning back, looking at the ceiling, perhaps taking the moment to relax a bit. Whenever the safety manager asked for engaging input, no one said anything.

Then there was an update on the recovery of one of their team members at a sister site.

The room changed instantly. People sat up straighter. Someone asked how he was doing. Another wanted to know what had happened. Questions came quickly, overlapping. It turned into a collaborative little incident conversation, everyone trying to piece together the details and understand whether he'd be okay.

No one had told them to pay attention. No one had asked them to care. They just did, because this was someone they knew.

The contrast was striking. Minutes earlier, "look out for each other" had been abstract words that slid past without friction. Now, with a specific person in mind, accountability became immediate and personal. The work mattered because he mattered.

Belonging makes accountability mutual. When you feel connected to the people around you, you don't want to be the reason someone gets hurt. You don't want to set a bad example. You don't want to let your crew down.

Safety is often framed as individual responsibility, but it rests on relationships. People commit to what they feel part of.

Questions that bring this to the surface include:

- "Who relies on you to do this well?"
- "Who have you relied on when things got difficult?"
- "What's a moment when someone's care for you made a difference?"

Living up to how you see yourself

The work matters because it reflects who you are or want to be.

When I asked one of the line workers what made his job meaningful, he didn't talk about rules, audits, or targets. He talked about how the work looked when it was finished.

"There's something about standing back and seeing a completed job," he said. "When the pole is straight, the cross arm is square, and the fittings are clean, it looks right. That pole might be there for fifty years, and I had a hand in that."

For him, quality wasn't an abstract standard. It was a signature. Anyone who knew the work could see it immediately. A job done well announced itself, but a rushed or careless one did too. Over time, that sensitivity followed him everywhere. "It's a professional disease," he joked. "I can't drive past a pole anymore without judging it."

What's striking is that no one was policing him. There was no supervisor checking every bolt, no procedure that could capture the difference between work that merely passed inspection and work that carried pride. The standard lived somewhere else.

"We're accountable to ourselves here," he said. "No one is telling us to do a good job. We do it that way because that's how we want to be seen."

That sense of identity shaped his everyday decisions in subtle ways, from taking an extra few minutes to line something up properly, to redoing a small section rather than leaving it "good enough". Or from speaking up when a shortcut would quietly undermine the finish, not because a rule demanded it, but because letting it slide would chip away at something he cared about.

He also knew that others were watching. Apprentices learned what mattered not from induction sessions, but from what experienced workers were willing to accept from themselves. Every compromise taught a lesson. So did every correction. "If I walk past something sloppy," he said, "I'm telling the next bloke that this is okay. And that's not the sort of tradesman I want to be."

This is what accountability looks like when it's anchored in identity rather than compliance. Behaviour aligns not because someone is enforcing it, but because acting otherwise would be out of step with how a person sees themselves, and how they want their work to speak for them long after they've moved on.

When expectations align with how people see themselves or aspire to be, compliance becomes self-expression. Following the standard isn't about avoiding consequences, it's about being the kind of person you want to be.

Questions that bring this to the surface include:

- "What kind of professional do you want to be?"
- "What do you want to be known for?"
- "When do you feel proud of how you showed up?"

From expectations to commitment

There are probably more dimensions than the six listed above. These are simply the currents I've encountered most often in practice. They're ways that meaning shows up in real conversations.

These currents rarely appear in isolation. A single accountability conversation might touch several at once, such as concern for a colleague, pride in craft, a sense of professional identity, and an awareness of downstream consequences. What matters is not naming the current, but sensing which ones are already present and helping them come into view.

This is where accountability becomes less about enforcement and more about recognition. You're helping them see how what's being asked already connects to what they care about, who they care about, and how they want to show up in their work.

> Accountability conversations don't make expectations softer, but they do make them deeper.

That's why accountability conversations can feel surprisingly light when they land well. Not because the standard is weak, but because the resistance has nowhere to stand. The conversation isn't pushing against the person, it's aligning with them. Seen this way, accountability is something you help people step into. But they can only step into it if you're actually standing on the same ground.

Standing on the same ground

Accountability conversations are about the future. They ask people to step into a shared direction and to stand behind what will happen next. But that step can't be taken unless people are standing on the same ground.

Too often, leaders assume alignment is a given because a message has been delivered. The plan has been explained and the expectation has been stated, so silence is taken as agreement. But understanding and commitment are not the same thing. People may nod while privately carrying doubt, disbelief, or a different picture of what is being asked.

Before accountability can be meaningful, it needs a brief pause to check whether the ground is stable enough to move forward together. It is about discovering whether shared commitment is possible.

A simple check-in can make the difference between willing accountability and quiet compliance.

Leaders who do this well ask questions that test shared understanding rather than loyalty. They stay curious about how the message has landed, not just how it was delivered.

Questions like the following often open the conversation:

- "What part of this feels clear, and what feels uncertain?"
- "From where you sit, does this direction seem workable?"
- "What feels unrealistic or missing?"
- "What matters to you in this?"

These questions strengthen authority and responsibility. They signal that accountability is something we enter together, not something imposed from above.

Sometimes the check-in reveals genuine alignment. People see the same future and are ready to commit. Other times it reveals differences that need attention before moving on, such as a concern that hasn't been spoken, a constraint that has been underestimated, or a purpose that hasn't yet been shared.

Accountability built on unspoken doubt rarely holds. Accountability built on shared understanding has a different quality. People follow through because they recognise themselves in what is being asked, not because they are being watched.

This moment of checking the ground is small, but it matters. It is where sensemaking turns forward. It is where people decide, often quietly, whether this is a future they are willing to stand behind.

Only when that choice is visible does accountability become real.

Inviting accountability

Accountability conversations are about creating the conditions where responsibility can be stepped into, rather than pushed back or performed.

At some point, accountability requires clarity. This usually means naming what you observed, without interpretation or assumed intent.

I've heard effective accountability conversations start with simple factual statements, such as, "When I walked past just now, I noticed the guard wasn't on the angle grinder." Or, "Around 9am yesterday I saw the scissor lift being operated without a spotter."

The precision matters. It anchors the conversation in observable reality rather than judgement or character. It's harder to defend against a fact than an interpretation.

Making impact visible means widening the frame – helping the person see how this moment connects to others who depend on their work, to downstream consequences they might not have considered, to the trust relationships they've built, to how they see themselves professionally, or to the responsibilities they want to carry in the future. This is about making meaning visible. Accountability deepens when people can see why a standard matters, not just that it exists.

To bring in the partnership approach from Chapter 4, what seems to help is inviting the person to shape the solution with you. For example:

- "Given all this, what do you think needs to happen?"
- "What does 'done properly' look like from your perspective?"
- "What would make this safe and workable from your side?"

Accountability doesn't end when the conversation feels good. Sometimes it helps to stay with what follows. For example:

- "What support do you need from me?"
- "When will this be sorted?"
- "How will we know it's done?"

These are ways of honouring the seriousness of the moment without slipping back into surveillance. This keeps accountability practical without slipping back into control.

Commitment that lasts beyond supervision

The approach outlined in this chapter changes what accountability feels like. It replaces public shaming with clarity, disciplinary measures with shared meaning, and compliance theatre with ownership.

When accountability conversations are handled this way, people reconnect with why their work matters, who it affects, and what kind of professional they want to be.

When Hugh connected wearing a hard hat to the team's future, to trust, and to professional identity, he transformed an expectation into a commitment. The worker didn't comply because he was being watched; he committed because he recognised himself in what was being asked.

Accountability conversations don't make expectations softer, but it does make them deeper. They turn rules into responsibilities, and responsibilities into commitments that last beyond supervision. People follow through because they recognise themselves in what's being asked.

CHAPTER 9
Restorative Conversations

There are moments in organisational life when something essential has been strained or broken between people. Perhaps a decision landed badly, a promise was missed, or an incident shook confidence. Someone felt blamed, ignored, or was left carrying something alone. Work may continue, but the ground beneath it is no longer steady.

Restorative conversations are much needed in the wake of such moments. Their purpose is simple and foundational – to repair the human ground that allows people to work together with trust, dignity, and confidence.

When that ground is damaged, people protect themselves. They become careful with their words, they may offer partial stories, or they comply without committing. The system may move on, but people don't. And when people are guarded, learning stalls, accountability becomes brittle, and improvement efforts struggle to take hold.

Restoration is necessary workplace care. It's pre-work for work to flow again.

Restorative conversations attend first to how an experience has landed for someone. They create space for what has been held, felt, or carried quietly to be spoken. When that happens, tension softens, perspective widens, and people no longer face the situation alone. Only then does it become possible to make sense of what happened together, without fear or defensiveness.

A conversation that reopened what had been shut

One of the clearest examples I've seen of this came from my friend Ron Gantt, a safety leader I've worked alongside for years.

A major construction project had been shut down following a series of serious incidents. Work had stopped and the client was furious. The relationship between the principal contractor and a key subcontractor had collapsed into open blame. Meetings had become rigid and adversarial, and people spoke carefully, if at all. Trust, once assumed, had drained away.

When the principal contractor announced they were sending their HSE director from the United States to "help address the situation", the subcontractor's leadership braced for impact. They expected an audit, findings, and consequences.

When Ron phoned ahead to introduce himself, the subcontractor's head of safety didn't soften the message. "This is a bad idea," he said. "You're going to make things worse."

For close to an hour, the head of safety spoke without interruption. He spoke about pressure, blame, feeling set up to fail, exhaustion, and about how every conversation now felt like a trap. Ron didn't correct the story or offer his own version. He stayed with it, letting the weight of it land.

When Ron arrived on site a few days later, he didn't come with a plan, a checklist, or an agenda.

At the opening meeting, he began in an unexpected way. "I'm not here to assign blame or issue findings. I'm here to understand, and if at any point this conversation stops being useful, you're free to step out."

There was a pause. People waited for the follow-up, the hidden condition, or the moment when authority would assert itself. It didn't come.

What arrived instead was choice.

Ron began with a simple question: "Can you tell me about a time on this project that has been most frustrating for you?"

At first, responses were cautious. Then one supervisor spoke, then another. Stories emerged about schedules that couldn't be met, concerns that went unanswered, and inspection scores that had dropped sharply in a single month.

"That felt like punishment," one person said.

Ron listened, then shared what he had heard from the safety team responsible for the inspections. The intention had been to draw attention to a growing risk, not to punish. Until that moment, neither side had fully heard the other.

People began to see that while harm had been done, it had not been intended. They weren't enemies. Instead, they were caught in a system that translated pressure into blame and concern into control.

By the end of the day, there were no new procedures, corrective actions, or a formal close-out. But conversation had become possible again. The group agreed to keep meeting, not to review metrics, but to talk about how the work was unfolding and what was making it harder than it needed to be. Trust began to return because people no longer felt alone inside it.

When restorative conversations are needed

In a small group conversation, one person kept circling back to the same issue, no matter what question was asked, and no matter what his colleagues brought up. At first it felt obstructive and unhelpful. The story on repeat was that the issue he'd raised many times had never been acted on. It was impossible for the person to move on because nothing had moved underneath them.

There was unfinished business. Until that experience was acknowledged, no new learning was possible. The conversation was stuck because something unresolved was still asking to be seen.

You need restoration when:

- people are guarded or unusually careful
- the same issue keeps resurfacing
- conversations feel brittle or tense
- someone is carrying something alone
- trust has thinned, even if work continues
- emotion shows up where logic was expected.

These are diagnostic signals that tell you that restoration, not analysis, is the work in front of you. When you recognise these moments, the question becomes, "How do you create the conditions where repair is possible?"

Restoration has a rhythm, and timing matters more than most people realise. Move too quickly and you risk re-injuring someone who is not yet ready. Wait too long and the distance becomes harder to close.

There is no perfect formula, but there are patterns worth noticing.

Immediately after a difficult event, people are often in acute distress. They may exhibit shock, anger, confusion, or numbness. In that state, restoration is not yet possible because people can't yet think clearly about what they need or what repair might look like.

If you try to have a restorative conversation while someone is still in the grip of strong emotion, it can feel like you're trying to make yourself feel better rather than attending to them. They may say things they don't mean or agree to things they can't commit to, just to end the discomfort.

A rough guide is to wait until the intensity has passed. That might be a few hours, or it might be a few days. You'll know they are ready when they can talk about what happened without being flooded by it.

There is a window after the initial shock settles but before people have fully adjusted to the new distance between them. This is the moment when restoration has the best chance of landing.

You can sense this window when someone seems able to reflect rather than just react. When they can say "I was really upset" rather than still being visibly upset. When they are open to hearing your perspective, even if they don't agree with it yet.

If you're unsure, you can test readiness gently. For example, "I know last week was hard. I would like to talk about it when you're ready. Does now feel okay, or would you prefer a bit more time?"

Sometimes the moment passes. They may have already made their decision, mentally or literally, and they have moved on, moved out, or moved into a stance of permanent guardedness.

You can still attempt restoration at this stage, but it's harder. The relational ground has already shifted, and people have often built protections that are difficult to undo.

If you find yourself here, the conversation might sound different. For example, "I know we haven't talked about what happened, and I realise it might be too late to fully repair things, but I wanted to say what I wish I'd said then ..."

Sometimes that is enough. Not to restore the relationship, but to give both people a sense of closure.

Before initiating a restorative conversation, check in with yourself. Are you genuinely ready to hear their experience, even if it's hard? Or are you still defending your actions internally? If you're not ready, wait. A half-hearted attempt at restoration often does more harm than good.

For the other person, watch for small signals. Are they making eye contact again? Are they willing to be in the same room without visible tension? Have they mentioned the incident in passing, which might indicate they're ready to talk about it more fully?

If weeks or months have passed and you realise restoration never happened, it is still worth trying. It will be harder, but not impossible.

You might open with, "I know it's been a while since that situation, and we never really talked about it, but I've been thinking about it, and I wanted to see if you'd be willing to revisit it with me?"

Some people will be relieved. Others will have moved on and won't want to reopen it. Respect their choice.

Organisations often want to move quickly past difficult events. There is pressure to get back to normal, to put it behind everyone, to focus on the future. But people don't heal on organisational timelines. Someone might need more time than the system is willing to give.

If you're a leader, your job is to protect space for restoration, even when there is pressure to move on. That might mean saying to your own manager, "I know we want to close this out, but the relationship is still strained. If we don't attend to that now, it will cost us later."

> Restoration isn't always possible. But the attempt still matters because it signals that you care about the relationship and the person, even if repair is beyond reach.

And if you are the person who needs more time, it's okay to say so. For example, "I appreciate that the organisation is ready to move forward. I'm not quite there yet. I need a bit more time before I can fully engage again."

Restoration begins with your own willingness to feel uncomfortable, to hear what you might not want to hear, and to sit with the space between where you are and where you'd like to be. The conversation itself follows its own rhythm. Sometimes you need to create space before anything can be spoken, sometimes acknowledgement comes before understanding, and sometimes the work is simply staying present while someone decides whether they can trust you again. The sequence isn't formulaic because the hurt isn't formulaic. What you can offer is steadiness, honesty, and the genuine desire to repair what's been damaged, because you care enough to keep showing up.

The limits of restoration

Restoration is powerful, but it isn't magic! There are times when conversation alone can't repair what has been damaged. Recognising those limits is part of working with integrity.

Some breaches of trust are catastrophic and the betrayal has cut so deep that the relationship can't recover. If someone has been deliberately harmed, repeatedly let down, or fundamentally misled, restoration may not be possible.

However, you can still offer the conversation. You can still take responsibility for your part. But you can't expect the other person to meet you there. They may need to protect themselves by maintaining distance, and that is their right.

Sometimes you reach out and the other person isn't willing to talk. They might say they're fine when they clearly are not. They might avoid you, or they might agree to meet and then cancel.

You can't force restoration. If someone isn't ready or willing, respect that boundary. You can leave the door open by saying, "I understand you don't want to talk about this right now. If that changes, I'm here." But don't keep pushing as that becomes its own form of harm.

Sometimes the problem isn't primarily relational, it's structural, such as impossible workloads, incompatible role expectations, or resource scarcity that puts people in competition with each other.

You can restore the personal relationship, but if the system keeps creating the same pressures, the strain will return. In those cases, restoration needs to be accompanied by systemic change, or it won't hold.

Sometimes repair requires action and not just dialogue. For example, a change in how work is allocated, a shift in decision-making authority, or a restructure that removes people from direct conflict.

If that's true, name it. For example, "I think we can improve how we work together, but I also think the reporting structure is part of what is creating tension. We need to address both."

Conversation can clarify what needs to change, but it can't substitute for making the change.

Not every restorative conversation will return the relationship to what it was. Sometimes the best you can do is establish a workable professional relationship, even if the warmth or trust is gone.

That is still worth doing because people don't need to be friends to collaborate effectively. They just need enough relational ground to communicate honestly and coordinate their work.

If you've made a genuine effort at restoration and it hasn't shifted anything, you have a few choices:

- You can try again later, with a different approach or at a different time.
- You can accept that this is as good as it will get and focus on managing the relationship professionally.
- You can recognise that separation is the kindest option for everyone involved.

Restoration isn't always possible. But the attempt still matters because it signals that you care about the relationship and the person, even if repair is beyond reach.

Restoration after incidents

Incidents place people under immediate strain. Shock, fear, guilt, anger, and confusion often arrive before any coherent account of what happened. In those moments, the most important work is steadiness.

Early contact after an incident is about helping people feel safe enough to settle. When that happens, their capacity to think returns.

Restorative contact is simple and human. It looks like sitting with someone before asking what happened, checking how they're doing before checking what they did, and making it clear that the person matters more than the timeline. "Are you okay?" comes before "What went wrong?"

Once people are no longer in acute distress, a different kind of conversation becomes possible. It's an opportunity for experience to be spoken rather than held. When that happens, tension softens and dignity returns.

Organisations often reverse this order. They rush to understand what went wrong while people are still shaken, guarded, or ashamed. In those conditions, stories flatten and defensiveness appears because the ground isn't yet safe enough to stand on.

Restorative conversations don't replace investigation, accountability, or improvement, but they prepare people for them. They allow learning to land where it otherwise can't.

What restoration gives back to the system

When restorative conversations are handled well, people become more willing to speak honestly about pressure and trade-offs. Hidden constraints surface, assumptions soften, and leaders hear more of the truth. Learning becomes possible when people feel safe enough to think and talk together.

But restoration does more than repair individual relationships – it changes how the organisation relates to itself.

Each time someone takes the risk of naming what has been difficult – and that risk is met with steadiness rather than defensiveness – the organisation becomes a slightly safer place for truth. Each time a leader acknowledges harm without deflecting, the distance between roles softens. Each time restoration happens, the "we" that makes other conversations possible grows stronger.

This is how the relational ground beneath safety is maintained. It's not through policies or programs, but through the willingness to repair what has been strained before moving on.

The six conversation types we have explored – connection, learning, appreciation, possibility, accountability, and restoration – are the building blocks of organisational dialogue. But individual moments, however skilful, aren't enough. The questions that follow are: How do these moments become movements? How does conversational practice spread beyond individual skill to become the way an organisation works?

That is what we turn to next.

PART THREE

From Moments to Movements

CHAPTER 10

Building a Conversational Organisation

The technician had been looking for a thermometer for five days. Just a basic thermometer to measure hangar temperature so he could calculate cable tension on the aircraft. You don't guess cable tension.

I was spending time with aircraft technicians at a regional airline. Base maintenance had been outsourced to a contractor while line maintenance remained in-house. They shared the same hangar, but not easily. There was rivalry, a little resentment, and competition for scarce resources. Tools "walked" between bays, equipment was borrowed but not returned, and people protected what they had because no one else would.

The technicians I spoke with were skilled and committed, but the system made even basic tasks hard. Training support was inconsistent, equipment was patchy, work was behind schedule, and safety incidents kept appearing. They improvised more than they wanted to because it had become the only way to keep the work moving.

In the middle of our conversation, one of them mentioned something that sounded small but caught my attention. He said, almost offhandedly, "There are so many tools and equipment problems. One simple thing is a thermometer. Just a normal thermometer to measure the temperature in the workshop for cable tension. I've been looking and asking around for five days. Can't find it."

I didn't fill the silence. I wanted to see where he would go.

His voice softened, as if naming the workaround exposed something he wasn't sure should be spoken. "I eventually used the iPhone to get the temperature."

There was a flicker of embarrassment, maybe even vulnerability, before frustration took over. Not at what he'd done, but at the fact that this was the only option the system had left him.

From there, more stories surfaced. Missing tools, unreliable equipment, messy parts stores with faulty inventory lists ... What shouldn't be hard had become unnecessarily difficult. And beneath these frustrations sat something more fragile – a fracture between line and base maintenance that nobody was naming directly.

Later, when I shared the technician's quote with senior managers, the room changed. Some looked shocked while others nodded slowly, recognising something they had suspected but not quite seen. The thermometer helped them recalibrate, to acknowledge openly how far reality had drifted from expectation.

The thermometer didn't travel because I decided it should. It travelled because it carried something people recognised immediately, which was the gap between what the system claims or aspires to, and the experience of the work. The story travelled because it was simple, human, and hard to ignore. It didn't need exaggeration because it carried its own weight.

And once spoken, it provided language that others could use without sounding negative or confrontational. Stories do that remarkably well. They make it easier to talk about what was previously difficult to say, and they form the bridge between moments and movements.

That's what this chapter is about. Not the thermometer itself, but what happens when individual conversational moments like this accumulate, travel, and eventually transform how an organisation understands itself. It's about moving from isolated insights to systemic change. From moments to movements, and from conversations to a conversational organisation.

When a moment starts to move

Let's say you just had a conversation that mattered. Something emerged that hadn't been named before, such as a technician spending five days looking for a thermometer, a workaround that revealed a design problem, or a small truth that only appeared because the conversation was different this time.

Then the conversation ended. You walked away, the work continued, and on the surface, nothing changed. The insight stayed with you, but you weren't sure what to do with it.

This is the moment many people find difficult. What do you do next? What do you pass on, if anything? Is what you've learned meaningful? Would people be receptive? It's small data, and not very evidence-heavy or impressive.

What emerges in conversations is often not a problem with a solution attached, or a new best practice ready to be spread and implemented. What you learnt may feel off, but not clearly wrong; a tension you can sense but can't yet name. The technician's thermometer story wasn't an immediate safety issue. It was a topic that had come up spontaneously when I'd come to site to understand working-at-height challenges. Was it signal, or noise, in relation to my inquiry?

Many parts of what he told me felt significant and important – the five days of searching, the embarrassment when naming his workaround, the frustration underneath. While too early to say, I knew I had to get other people to hear it, reflect on it, and decide.

Recognising significance

Not every conversation produces insights that need to travel. Most conversations are exactly what they appear to be: coordination, clarification, connection. The challenge is developing judgement about when something matters beyond the immediate moment.

What made the thermometer story significant was what the thermometer revealed, which was a gap between expectation and reality, a pattern of workarounds, a fractured relationship creating operational risk, and workers carrying burdens they shouldn't have to carry alone.

You're likely holding something significant when the story carries emotion, holds tension or contradiction, when the person telling it seems vulnerable or hesitant, when it connects to other stories you've heard, when it makes you think, *If this is true here, where else might it be true?*, and when you can't stop thinking about it after the conversation ends.

The thermometer became significant not in the moment, he told me, but in the moment I recognised what it was pointing towards.

The responsibility of holding truth

Once you recognise significance, you're carrying something. It's not just information or insight, but someone's trust. The technician didn't have to tell me about the iPhone workaround – he chose to. That choice came with the risk of looking incompetent, of getting in trouble, and of nothing changing anyway.

When someone takes that risk you become at least partly responsible for what happens to their story.

This responsibility sits uncomfortably, at least with me. You may not have the authority to fix what they've described, you may not even know if it should be fixed, and you certainly can't guarantee that sharing their story will lead to change.

But doing nothing, letting the insight die in silence, feels like a betrayal of the trust people have offered.

I sat with the thermometer story for several days. I knew it mattered, but I wasn't certain what to do with it. I couldn't fix the tool shortage myself. I wasn't managing the base maintenance contract. I didn't control resource allocation. What I could do was help the story reach people who needed to hear it. But that required care.

Letting insight travel

When you decide an insight needs to move beyond you, the question becomes: How do you carry it forward without losing what made it matter?

Creating containers

Insight needs a form that can travel. You can't replay whole conversations, and even if you had transcripts, they would be too long, too messy, and too risky to share. The technician's full frustration, his colleagues chiming in, the ambient sense of the hangar, none of that can be packaged neatly.

What you can do is distil the essence without losing what matters. You can cut out the fragments that carry what you've learned.

For the thermometer story, the container was simple: his exact words, minimal context, and the question it raised.

When I spoke with senior managers, I had put the technician's quote on a slide. I said, "I spent time with your technicians last week. Here's what one of them told me." And then I showed the quote.

I didn't elaborate. I didn't interpret. I let the story sit.

What makes stories travel

Not all stories travel. Some stay exactly where they were told, while others spread through an organisation like wildfire.

The thermometer story travelled because it was concrete, recognisable, and carried its own weight. It didn't require people to trust my analysis. It simply asked them to sit with a reality they could immediately recognise.

Stories that travel tend to share certain qualities:

- They're specific and human, not abstract. The thermometer, five days, the iPhone workaround, the embarrassment – they're details that paint a picture.
- They're emotionally honest. The technician's vulnerability came through, so did his frustration. People respond to that honesty.
- They have tension or a point. Some reveal gaps between aspiration and reality. Most corporate managers operated on the assumption that maintenance crews had the tools they

needed. The thermometer showed that belief was wrong. Other stories bring across other surprises and gaps, whether they're relational, informational, task related, or emergent practices.
- They invite recognition, not defensiveness. The story didn't blame anyone. It simply described what was, which made it safer to acknowledge.

When a story has these qualities, you don't have to push it. It moves easily on its own because people recognise the value when they hear it.

When sharing goes wrong

Sometimes stories don't land the way you hoped. You share something you thought was significant, and people dismiss it, minimise it, or get defensive.

This can happen for many reasons, such as the timing being wrong, the audience not being ready to hear it, your relationship with them not being strong enough to carry difficult truth, or the story itself not travelling as well as you thought it would.

When this happens, you have choices. You can try again later with different framing, you can find a different audience, or you can accept that this insight isn't going to move right now and let it go.

What you shouldn't do is force it. Pushing too hard damages trust and makes future sharing less likely to succeed. Sometimes the most responsible thing is to hold the insight quietly until conditions shift.

A technician once told me, "I know things aren't right here, and I've tried to tell my supervisor, but he doesn't want to hear it. I've put it in the reporting system, but I never hear back from anyone, so I've stopped trying."

When the system can't receive truth, people learn to stop offering it. That's a cost worth avoiding.

When patterns gain weight

Individual stories matter, but when multiple stories start revealing the same underlying issue, something begins shifting. What was anecdotal becomes undeniable, and what felt like an isolated problem reveals itself as systemic.

This is what happened at the airline. The thermometer wasn't the only story. Over several weeks of conversations, a pattern emerged of missing equipment and tools, plans and permissions that were late, new tasks that no one had seen before, work delays, and improvised workarounds. Each story was small, but together they painted a picture of a system struggling to support the people working in it.

To make this pattern more visible we set up a "collaborative sensemaking" session. This wasn't just with a few technicians, but with an invite to a representative cross-section of the people affected, including maintenance crews, supervisors, operational managers, people from HR, planning, tools stores, and senior managers from head office.

Making patterns visible

We collected stories from across the site beforehand. Not through surveys or questionnaires, but through conversations. I spoke with people about their work, asking what was going well, what was difficult, what they wished leadership understood. Those conversations were printed verbatim, one story per page, anonymised but unedited.

On the day of the session, we covered the walls of a large room with these stories. There were over a hundred pages. The room looked chaotic at first with stories everywhere, voices layered on top of each other.

The room fell quiet as people moved along the walls, reading and pairing up with colleagues they didn't usually work with. I asked them to notice what seemed to be helping, and what was making work harder than it needed to be. They attached their comments to the page, signalling it had been read, and moved on to read more.

Within an hour, a picture emerged that no one could have seen alone. It didn't appear through data or dashboards, but through the organisation's own voice made visible. We gathered around to reflect on what they had just read. I was keen to hear how it all landed.

"It's a mess!"

"We're a whiney bunch."

"But this is what it's like here."

No one dismissed what was presented. The most senior manager from head office didn't say anything, but he looked rather pale. He was seeing his operation through a completely different lens.

People recognised their own words. They saw their isolated frustration reflected in others' experiences. They began connecting dots: "The story about missing equipment, that's why the turnaround was late in this other story." The pattern that emerged wasn't "technicians are struggling with tools". There were several systemic gaps and discontinuities, not something that had a specific root cause, but many contributory factors.

I asked them to go back to the walls and start organising the pages into clusters. Each cluster had a tight connection between the stories, together illustrating a bigger challenge. One hundred pages got organised into twelve themes, and from there we went on to try to define the challenge, giving it a heading, an impact statement, a problem statement, and some suggested improvement ideas if they came up in the discussion.

It gave the site, and corporate, something to work with. Twelve named challenges with shared understanding of what was creating them, and a shared incentive and capability to do something about it. But seeing the pattern was just the beginning.

When recognition creates movement

Something powerful happens when people see patterns collectively rather than individually. It's no longer "I think there's a problem" but "We can all see this is happening."

In the room that day, the shift was palpable. Technicians stopped feeling like they were complaining or being blamed and started feeling heard. Managers stopped feeling like they were being attacked and started feeling curious. The challenge was shared, and so was the opportunity and interest to do something about it.

When patterns become visible, blame becomes less interesting than understanding.

What helps patterns emerge

You don't create patterns; they exist whether you notice them or not. Your role is to help make them visible.

What seems to matter is collecting across contexts, staying curious about repetition, resisting the urge to name things too quickly, creating spaces for collective seeing, and trusting that patterns will emerge when they're ready to, rather than trying to force them.

The thermometer was never just about the thermometer. It was a thread, a piece of a mosaic. When followed carefully, with others, it led to something larger that the whole organisation needed to see.

However, sustainable change requires more than one pattern-recognition workshop. The airline didn't just need to see these twelve challenges once. They needed to develop the capacity to keep seeing themselves clearly, to create channels where truth could travel routinely, not just when a consultant facilitated it. They needed to build conversation into their infrastructure, not treat it as a temporary cure. This is what separates a moment of insight from genuine organisational transformation. This is what it means to become a conversational organisation.

What is a conversational organisation

Most of my work – when you strip away the methods and the travel and the diagrams on walls – has been remarkably simple. I listen to people. I collect their stories. I help them see what they already know, and then I hold those stories up to the organisation itself so it can finally recognise what has been right in front of it.

It's that simple, and that difficult.

It is the work of helping an organisation relate to itself in a fuller and more honest way. Sometimes this is obvious, sometimes it takes courage to name, and sometimes it's almost like therapy – the talking cure – not for individuals this time, but for organisations.

> I listen to people. I collect their stories. I help them see what they already know, and then I hold those stories up to the organisation itself so it can finally recognise what has been right in front of it.

The idea of conversation as a form of cure isn't new. When Sigmund Freud and Josef Breuer began treating patients through dialogue rather than physical intervention, one patient famously described the process as "the talking cure". What mattered was creating space for what had been unspoken to be named, integrated, and worked through.

Organisations are not so different. I don't mean this therapeutically – organisations aren't patients – but like therapy, conversational work creates conditions where what's been hidden can finally be acknowledged, integrated, and worked with. The breakdowns we see in safety, culture, and performance often come from the same source – realities that have nowhere to go, pressures that can't be acknowledged, contradictions that can't be spoken about. Tensions that travel underground because there is no safe place for them above the surface.

When an organisation can't talk to itself, it can't know itself. And when it can't know itself, it can't make sense of what's happening or take responsible action. It starts to compensate with controls, rules, initiatives, campaigns, and rhetoric. The tools can create structure, but they can't help an organisation reflect on itself; that work happens in relationship.

The airline that I worked with exemplifies this journey. When I first met them, they were stuck in a familiar pattern of corporate mandates, site resistance, repeated performance challenges, frustration, and more corporate mandates. Then, within months of their first genuine conversation with site-based personnel at a particularly problematic site, things had shifted dramatically. The site went from problem child to poster child. More importantly, the way they related to themselves as an organisation transformed. Site and corporate were pulling in the same direction. The change lasted years.

Over the course of this book, you may have noticed a pattern. Each time an organisation struggles to understand its own safety, it reaches for something to stabilise, such as a metric, a model, a process, or a story it can repeat. These things aren't wrong, and in fact they're necessary. Without them, work would be impossible to coordinate.

The trouble begins when these representations stop moving, when the tools we use to simplify reality become mistaken for reality itself, or when the stories that once helped us make sense of work begin to crowd out the experience of the people doing it.

Conversations work differently. They aren't designed to travel far or last long. They are situated, incomplete, and often uncomfortable. But they have one crucial property – they keep the organisation in contact with itself.

A conversational organisation is not one that avoids standards or structure. It is one that treats its ways of understanding as provisional. One that expects its picture of the work to be revised by those closest to it, and one that keeps the cost of reframing low, so that new signals can be taken seriously before they become failures.

This isn't about having better questions, or the right answers. It is about staying with the questions long enough for the system to remain thinkable by the people inside it. A conversational organisation is one that has learned to resist the drift towards "us and them".

Most organisations manage distance through control systems, but as we saw with Transpower and throughout this book, conversation offers a different path – it closes distance through relationship rather than managing it through structure. A conversational organisation uses dialogue to maintain connection across hierarchy, building "we" rather than reinforcing separation.

This doesn't mean the organisation is flat or informal or slow. It means that real, honest, two-way conversation is treated as essential infrastructure. Not as a nice-to-have or a culture initiative, but as the primary mechanism through which the organisation stays in contact with itself.

Learning to see itself

A conversational organisation relates to itself through people, lived experience, stories that carry texture and contradiction, and through moments where someone says something that shifts the room from posturing into truth.

In these moments, the organisation becomes aware of itself. It gains a kind of inner coherence. It sees how its processes, expectations, and structures are shaping real work. It recognises how its competing priorities are shaping behaviour, and it notices where it is creating pressures it didn't intend.

A supervisor mentions pressure from two competing priorities, and someone from another team says, "We are feeling that same squeeze." What seemed like a local problem reveals itself as systemic.

A safety manager hears how a procedure creates risk instead of reducing it, and rather than defending the procedure, asks, "What would make this actually work?"

A conversational organisation has developed the capacity to see itself clearly enough to act differently. Think back to Deepwater Horizon (which we explored in Chapter 2). The day before it exploded, four senior executives walked the rig. They inspected housekeeping, checked PPE tags, discussed hand injury campaigns, and congratulated the crew on seven years' lost-time-injury-free. Everything looked as it should and everyone had the right answers. The leaders were engaged, observant, and sincere.

Yet the system couldn't see itself. The conversations happening on the rig – the information that mattered most – had no channel to reach those four executives. The walkaround touched the surface but never reached the depths where risk was living. There was no "we" strong enough to carry difficult truths across the distance between leadership and the drilling crew.

Now contrast that with what happened at Transpower. After years of attempting to bring about change through tightening controls, everyone was frustrated by the lack of improvement. The system was becoming increasingly frail and brittle.

Despite waning performance, the focus was on control, compliance, and progress, not on how the work was actually unfolding. Decisions were made with only part of the picture.

That changed when leaders began to listen differently. Instead of asking whether the program was on track, they asked how the work was really being done. Stories from the field were invited rather than filtered. When painters described the trade-offs they were making, those stories weren't treated as problems to fix locally, but as signals about the system itself.

As those stories began to move, patterns became visible. What had looked like isolated incidents of non-compliance revealed themselves as symptoms of systemic pressure. The organisation started to see how its own structures were creating the very risks it was trying to eliminate.

This capacity to see itself clearly didn't arrive through better reporting systems or more sophisticated analysis. It arrived through conversation, through people turning towards each other with honesty and being met with curiosity rather than judgement.

Every time an organisation learns to face one of these realities without flinching, it grows a little wiser. It develops tolerance for complexity and ambiguity, and it learns that seeing clearly is more valuable than maintaining comfortable fictions.

A higher tolerance for reality

Conversational organisations develop an unusual capacity: they can hold difficult truths without immediately rushing to resolve them.

This is harder than it sounds. Most organisations are action oriented. When a problem surfaces, the instinct is to fix it quickly, assign responsibility, and implement a solution. That instinct isn't wrong, but it can short-circuit understanding.

Sometimes the most valuable thing an organisation can do is sit with reality long enough to understand it fully before trying to change it.

At the airline, this showed up when leaders stopped treating every procedural breach as a compliance failure requiring immediate correction. Instead, they asked, "What is this breach telling us about the system?" Sometimes the answer was, "We have the wrong procedure." Or, "We have competing demands that we haven't acknowledged." Or, "We're asking people to do something that isn't actually possible within the constraints we've given them."

None of those insights would have emerged if the immediate response had been to enforce the standard.

This can feel like a leader admitting uncertainty without losing authority. It feels like a room of people acknowledging that they don't have all the answers and deciding to think together rather than defend their positions. It feels like someone saying, "I was wrong about that" and being respected for it rather than judged.

Over time, a conversational organisation becomes more familiar with its own messiness and more capable of working with it rather than against it.

What this tolerance looks like in practice:

- Leaders who can say "I don't know" without it being interpreted as weakness.

- Teams who can bring to the surface tensions and contradictions without needing to resolve them immediately.
- Systems that invite people to name problems even when solutions aren't clear.
- Conversations that can hold competing perspectives without forcing premature consensus.
- Processes that allow time for sensemaking, not just decision-making.

This ability grows slowly, mostly quietly, but it changes how the organisation responds to difficulty. Instead of defensiveness or denial, there's curiosity. Instead of blame, there's understanding. Instead of quick fixes that create new problems, there's thoughtful action based on deeper comprehension.

Becoming more itself

As conversational capacity grows, something shifts in the organisation's identity. It becomes less dependent on external consultants to tell it what it already knows. Less reliant on formal processes to surface reality. Less fragmented between those who do the work and those who design it.

The organisation starts to know itself better, not perfectly or completely, but more honestly than before.

This self-knowledge creates stability. This isn't the brittle stability of rigid control, but the adaptive stability of a system that can sense and respond to its own experience. When pressures build, the organisation can name them earlier. When things go well, it can understand why and protect those conditions. When change is needed, it has a clearer sense of what needs to change.

At the airline, this showed up in how they handled future challenges. Years after our initial work, they faced budget cuts and restructuring pressure. Instead of that triggering the old pattern of corporate mandate and site resistance, they convened conversations, they named the constraints honestly, and they involved people in thinking through trade-offs. The decisions that emerged weren't easy, but they were understood and accepted because people had been part of making sense of them.

The organisation had developed muscle memory for how to be honest with itself, even when the truth was difficult.

What a conversational organisation looks like

A conversational organisation doesn't look dramatically different on the surface. It still has hierarchies, procedures, metrics, and reporting structures. But the quality of what happens inside those structures changes. For example:

- Meetings become places where real thinking happens, not just updates and approvals.
- Leaders spend less time defending decisions and more time explaining the reasoning behind them.
- Problems arise earlier because people trust they'll be received with curiosity, not blame.
- Trade-offs are named and discussed rather than hidden or denied.
- Stories from the frontline shape decisions at senior levels.
- People across different levels and functions talk to each other as partners, not adversaries.
- When things go wrong, the first question is "What happened and what can we learn?" rather than "Who is responsible?"

- When things go well, the question becomes "What made this possible and how do we protect it?"

At the airline, I watched this play out over several years. The working-at-height breaches – the original problem that had seemed so intractable – largely disappeared. Not because procedures were enforced more strictly, but because the conversations revealed what was creating the risk. The organisation adjusted scaffolding availability, changed work planning, provided different equipment, and shifted how senior managers engaged with crews.

More importantly, the way people related to each other transformed. The site I initially worked with became known across the company as a place where things actually worked. Corporate started sending other struggling sites to learn from them to understand how they'd learned to talk to themselves honestly.

And they kept going. For years.

Even after I stopped working with them, the practice continued. It had become part of who they were, not just something they did when the consultant was watching.

Indicators of conversational health

How do you know if your organisation is developing this capacity? There are signals worth noticing:

- People bring forward problems early when they're still small and solvable, rather than hiding them until they become crises.
- Difficult conversations happen in real time, not in hallways afterwards or in closed-door complaints.

- When leaders ask, "What are you seeing?", people tell them honestly rather than what they think leaders want to hear.
- Meetings include genuine uncertainty and thinking together, not just presentations of pre-decided positions.
- Stories from frontline employees influence decisions at senior levels in visible, traceable ways.
- When something goes wrong, people's first instinct is to understand it rather than defend themselves from it.
- The language people use shifts from "they" and "them" to "we" when describing organisational challenges.
- People across hierarchical levels speak to each other with respect and genuine curiosity.
- New people joining the organisation notice and comment on the quality of conversation being different from other places they've worked.

No organisation has these qualities perfectly or consistently. But when you start noticing them happening more often, you're seeing conversational health developing.

How organisations grow this capacity

This doesn't happen accidentally, and it doesn't happen quickly. But it can be cultivated deliberately.

At the individual level

People need to develop their own conversational capacity through the skills we covered in earlier chapters: listening deeply, asking genuine questions, staying present with difficulty, appreciating what works, holding space for possibility, offering clear accountability, and restoring relationships when they fracture.

These aren't personality traits; they're practices that can be learned and strengthened through deliberate attention. Chapter 12 goes through this individual development in detail.

At the team level

Teams need regular space to reflect together on their work. Not just to report on it, but to make sense of it, to notice patterns, name tensions, and bring to the surface what's working and what isn't.

This might look like standing weekly debriefs that go beyond task status to ask, "How is the work actually going?" Or monthly learning conversations where teams deliberately examine both successes and struggles, or retrospectives after significant projects that genuinely explore what happened rather than just checking boxes.

The format matters less than the quality of attention and the regularity of practice.

At the organisational level

Leadership creates conditions where conversational practice can thrive or where it withers.

Every structural decision is also a relational decision:

- Do we design reporting systems that filter truth or channels that carry it?
- Do we create accountability mechanisms that drive defensiveness or invite honesty?
- Do we organise work in ways that fragment understanding or build shared sensemaking?
- Do we position frontline workers as problems to manage or partners to work with?

Leaders model and protect conversational practice when they ask genuine questions and stay with the answers, even when the answers are uncomfortable. Or when they convene conversations rather than just cascade messages. They create space for thinking together.

At the airline, this showed up when the head of maintenance began opening leadership meetings with, "What am I not seeing?" instead of, "Here's what we need to do." The shift was small but powerful. It signalled that leadership wanted truth, not confirmation.

Time also needs to be allocated for reflection and thinking together, not just delivery. Space in schedules and budgets that says, "This matters." Roles that focus on learning and sensemaking, not just compliance, help to institutionalise this.

The airline created dedicated time and a role for someone to support the improvement team. Not to run it, but to help it stay connected to other parts of the organisation, to capture what was being learned, and to protect the space from being turned into another compliance exercise.

Insights from the conversations feed into decisions, so the stories are influencing strategy, not just metrics. The frontline shapes the boardroom, not just the other way around. And when action isn't possible, explanation is given, such as, "Here is why we can't do that right now."

At the airline, every idea brought to the improvement team received a response within two weeks. Either, "We're trying this." "We can't do that because ..." or, "We need more information." The reliability of response kept people contributing.

What is genuinely helpful is the freedom for conversations to be messy, emergent and incomplete. Not polished for presentation, nor performed for cameras or documentation.

When the airline's executive team asked for metrics on the improvement team's impact, the site leader pushed back gently. "I can tell you stories about what has changed. I can show you the reduction in incidents and efficiency gains. But if you want me to count how many conversations we had, we'll stop having real ones." The executive team accepted the boundary.

The courage to turn towards what matters

Most organisations carry areas they struggle to see clearly. Certain truths might remain at the edges because they feel awkward or risky to name, such as chronic understaffing, impossible expectations, leadership blind spots, system design flaws, and the quiet gap between what is said and what is rewarded.

In safety, these realities often live inside everyday work. They are held by the people who know the job best, and they adapt around them, coping to make things work. And in doing so, they protect the organisation from seeing itself clearly.

A conversational organisation grows by turning towards these areas slowly and deliberately. Not by forcing exposure, but by creating conditions where difficult truths can be spoken when people are ready, and then received without defensiveness when they are.

In the airline story, what began as frustration with procedural breaches became a deeper inquiry into how the work was being done, and why. Leaders stopped jumping to solutions and started asking what the system was asking of people. Over time, the organisation learned how to understand itself better. This shared noticing changed how decisions were made. Risks were surfaced earlier, trade-offs became discussable, and action rested on a clearer picture of reality. Not because anyone had perfect information, but because the information that existed could finally move.

And the us/them fracture that had prevented understanding began to heal. Not completely and not everywhere, but enough that partnership became possible where there had been separation.

The work of integration

A conversational organisation is a practice. It is a way of being together that must be renewed constantly.

It grows every time someone chooses curiosity over defensiveness, presence over performance, and shared sensemaking over individual certainty. Every time a leader asks, "What are we not seeing?" instead of "Why is this not working?" Every time someone names a tension instead of working around it. Every time a story travels from the field to a decision room and shapes what happens next. Every time "How do we improve this?" replaces "How do I get you to do this?"

As this capacity develops, the work begins to feel different. People spend less time managing symptoms and more time understanding what those symptoms are pointing to. Conversations become places where issues can be named rather than avoided. Problems are brought forward earlier, when they are still soft enough to shape.

The us/them fracture, while never fully eliminated, stops being the default pattern. "We" becomes the way people think about their work together. Not through mandate or mission statement, but through the repeated, lived experience of being treated as partners rather than problems.

Safety starts to be shaped by this steady contact with reality, rather than by the next program or initiative. Not because programs don't matter, but because they work better when they rest on honest understanding of what people are navigating.

The most profound organisational change arrives through the quality of attention people bring to each other. It arrives when organisations stop managing symptoms and start listening to what those symptoms are trying to say. It arrives when conversation becomes a place where things that matter can finally be named.

And, as always, it begins in the simplest of ways: people turning to each other and asking, "What is really going on here? And how do we make it better together?"

I have spent years helping organisations develop conversational capacity. The work never looks the same twice. Every organisation has its own culture, constraints, and starting point. But the pattern is consistent: when people can talk honestly about their work – what makes it hard, what makes it possible, what would make it better – the organisation becomes more intelligent, more adaptive, and more humane.

This doesn't require perfection or everyone to become skilled facilitators. It requires enough people, at enough levels, willing to turn towards each other with curiosity and care, to ask real questions, to stay with difficulty, and willing to let truth reshape what they thought they knew.

Your organisation is having conversations right now – in meeting rooms and on job sites, in break rooms and on phone calls. The question is not whether conversation is happening. The question is whether those conversations are helping the organisation see itself clearly enough to learn, adapt, and improve.

CHAPTER 11

Conversational Safety Leadership

Traditional safety leadership manages organisational distance through control: stronger oversight, clearer expectations, and tighter accountability. As we've seen throughout this book, this deepens the us/them divide. Conversational leadership offers a different path, where you're building partnership through relationship rather than managing compliance through systems.

This doesn't mean abandoning authority or accountability. It means exercising them differently through conversation rather than control, partnership rather than enforcement, and shared sensemaking rather than top-down direction.

Every now and then I meet people who insist that what we need to improve safety is "strong and visible safety leadership". I usually understand the intention, that leaders should be seen doing the right things, but once you scratch the surface, the idea becomes vague. Strong in what way? Visible for what purpose?

Leading towards which future? And what exactly do we mean by "safety" in the first place?

When expanded, the "strong and visible" story tends to follow a familiar script:

- Leaders must set the standard and ensure everyone follows it.
- Leaders must draw the line in the sand.
- Leaders must be ready to have the tough conversations.

Put simply, this version of leadership relies on role-modelling, correction, and the use of rewards and punishments to secure compliance. It assumes that safety is achieved when deviations are eliminated, that people need to be nudged or pressured into doing the right thing, and that leadership is a matter of asserting authority.

This is classic transactional leadership, where leaders promote compliance by setting expectations and exchanging rewards or discipline for meeting or failing them. The focus stays on yesterday's rules and procedures rather than on curiosity, discovery, or adaptation.

There are several problems with this approach.

First, it treats safety as separate from work, as though risk appears only when people deviate, rather than being shaped by how work is designed, supported, and carried out. It confines leaders to a reactive posture, where improvement comes only from scanning for what went wrong. This produces a culture filled with deficits, threats, and negative attention, where nothing expands or grows.

Second, in a world of rapid technological change, global market competition, and constant cost pressures, leaders who cling to yesterday's answers risk slowing the organisation down. They discourage local insight and reduce initiative. They reinforce the unhelpful idea that people doing the work are there to follow instructions rather than to co-create a better future.

In 2023 I facilitated a workshop for emerging safety leaders. The CEO joined via video. He was sitting in his office but had put on his PPE shirt for the occasion. He spoke earnestly about safety as a core value, recited the main risks on site, and concluded by saying that leadership was all about "creating followership".

I remember thinking, *This is exactly the problem.* We don't need people who follow; we need people who can think, sense, adapt, and respond in ways no leader can predetermine. We need "fellowship" of people at all levels, working together towards a shared purpose.

Conversational leadership offers a different path, where leadership is built on shared discovery, mutual understanding, and working together to adapt and improve.

How conversational leadership works

When leadership is exercised through conversation, things change. Honesty increases, people stop competing for authority, collective intelligence emerges, and responsibility grows because people experience themselves as contributors. "Wwe" forms where there was fracture.

Conversational leadership begins with a simple but profound shift: leaders pay attention. They notice when the current trajectory isn't sustainable, when the story on the dashboard doesn't match the story on the ground, when frustrations are showing up in too many places at once, and when people are quietly adapting their way around a constraint that no one has named.

Noticing becomes leadership's first act. It calls out drift. It says, "We can't keep moving in this direction. We need to talk about this together."

Once a leader recognises that a conversation is needed, the work unfolds through six movements. These aren't steps to follow mechanically but ways of creating conditions where understanding can form.

Convene around questions that matter

Conversational leadership begins with bringing the right people together, or going to see the right people, and naming a real purpose. This isn't with answers, a slogan, or a corporate vision statement, but with a genuine question about work, tension, or possibility.

Shape the conditions

Leaders who rely on conversation do not fill the room with their expertise. They shape the conditions in which other people's expertise can surface. They pay attention to pace, openness, conditions for honesty, energy, and flow. They set the tone, not the script.

This is where "we" begins to form. Not because the leader declares it, but because the conditions allow it. When people feel connected enough to think aloud, when their perspective is genuinely sought, when the conversation isn't predetermined, then partnership becomes possible.

Help people see the system

Insights rarely arrive as neat conclusions. Instead, they show up in fragments: a story here, a frustration there, a contradictory experience from another corner of the organisation. Conversational leaders listen for these fragments and connect them. They help people see how their work fits with others, and they make tensions visible. They bring the system into the room so that people can reason together.

Protect honesty

Real conversation sometimes brings discomfort. Perhaps someone raises a difficult truth, a long-held frustration appears, or a vulnerability surfaces unexpectedly. Conversational leaders steady the room. They give the moment space without rushing, minimising, or fixing. They help people stay with the truth long enough for insight to emerge.

This is courage in action. Not the courage to enforce standards or have "tough conversations" about compliance, but the courage to stay present when reality doesn't fit the preferred narrative. To let "them" become visible as people navigating real constraints, not problems to solve.

Make the invisible visible

Leaders who listen well draw attention to what is emerging. They name small insights people might overlook, they reflect back patterns or themes the group is discovering, and they help the group see its own intelligence.

"I'm hearing that this issue shows up differently in three parts of the operation. What does that tell us?" This kind of noticing helps shared understanding form. It helps "we" see what "we" know together.

Close with momentum

Conversational leadership ends in a way that preserves momentum, naming what has shifted, identifying what still needs exploration, or acknowledging the clarity that has begun to form.

Have you noticed what's absent from these six movements? It's control. You're not controlling the content, the conclusions, or the outcomes. What you're creating are conditions where "we" can form, where people can think together across difference, hierarchy, and distance.

This is the fundamental shift conversational leadership requires: from controlling outcomes to creating conditions, from maintaining us/them through authority to building "we" through relationship.

What it looks like in practice

Kirsten, the site manager, was doing his usual walk around when he paused with one of the subcontractors and asked a simple question: "What ideas do you have for making things better or safer around here?"

The contractor hesitated, then said, "Well, just because you lot are different, I'll say something. On other sites I wouldn't bother because nothing ever happens. But here, I know you actually mean it." He pointed towards a container across the yard. "Those gas bottles in there. The access is really awkward. I have to stand on a thin ledge, and even then, I can barely reach the valves."

Instead of jumping to solutions, Kirsten walked over with him to have a look. She asked what it was like to handle the bottles day to day, what the contractor was trying to avoid, what he wished was easier. Together they trialled a few ideas: a mobile platform, a clearer turning circle, even the possibility of pouring a small concrete pad. They took photos, sketched options, and left with a shared sense of what "better" might look like.

A few weeks later, during a safety leadership coaching session, Kirsten told the story to her colleagues. You could see the realisation land as she spoke. It wasn't just interest in the improvement ideas, but pride in the way it came about. Her peers immediately picked up on it. "That's very host-like," one said. Others noted the real breakthrough in that crews were beginning to see the company as a place where conversation leads to change.

The COO, who was there that day, smiled and said, "This is exactly why we invest in this leadership work. To help you feel confident having conversations that let the truth come out, and that let people shape the solutions with you."

It was a small moment, but it showed what conversational leadership feels like in practice – not dramatic or heroic, but transformative, nevertheless. It didn't solve everything, but it changed the mood of the place, what was considered good, and desirable.

What Kirsten demonstrated was the shift from "How do I get contractors to work safely?" to "How do we make this work better together?" That question invited partnership, led to insights about the work, and shared ideas for a better workplace for everyone.

What changes when leaders lead conversationally?

When leaders begin to lead conversationally, the texture of organisational life shifts in subtle but unmistakable ways. Meetings stop feeling like reporting rituals, where people perform certainty or wait for the leader to decide. Instead, they become places where people think together. Less presentation, more exploration. Less "Any questions?" and more "What does this look like from your side?" As a result, reality can be spoken more easily without choreography.

Leaders show up differently too, speaking with less armour. They listen without rehearsing a response, and they ask questions that open space rather than fill it. And when they do, people stop bracing. The hierarchy is still present, but its weight softens. There is less pressure to impress and more permission to be real.

What might once have escalated into conflict arrives instead as small signals, such as a hesitation, a story, a comment that carries more than it says. Instead of defensiveness, there is curiosity, and instead of blame, there is shared problem-solving.

This allows people to take small interpersonal risks; they can admit uncertainty, name a tension, or share an example that once felt unsafe. When those vulnerable steps are met with steadiness rather than correction, confidence builds, as well as a practical sense that it is safe to approach a manager with what is awkward, unfinished, or uncomfortable.

As this capacity develops, the flow of work changes. Leaders spend less energy firefighting hidden issues and more time thinking with people about how work works. Conversations happen earlier, closer to where the work is done. You see people gathering, working things out before they become problems. There is more signal and less noise.

And perhaps the clearest sign is that conversations begin to happen without you. People initiate their own sensemaking. They raise tensions because it feels normal to do so. Responsibility becomes something people step into.

When leaders model "we"

The most powerful thing leaders can do is demonstrate what "we" looks like in practice. Not through speeches about collaboration, but through how they show up in conversations.

When a leader says, "I don't have the full picture. Help me understand," they're creating we. When a leader asks, "What are we not seeing?" they're inviting shared sensemaking. When a leader responds to frontline insight with, "That changes how I think about this," they're modelling that everyone's perspective matters. And when a leader says, "How do we make this work?" instead of "How do I get you to do this?" they're shifting the entire relational ground.

These are lived practices of partnership across hierarchy. And when leaders practise this consistently, it gives permission for others to do the same.

People notice when leaders show up differently, or when someone in authority admits uncertainty, asks genuine questions, and responds to challenge with curiosity rather than defence. It all signals that the old us/them patterns don't have to hold. People begin to test whether this is real by offering small pieces of truth to see what happens. When those truths are received well, they offer more.

Gradually, a different norm takes hold. Concerns are raised rather than buried, ideas are shared rather than held back, and people no longer relate to leadership defensively, but as partners in improving how the work is done.

This shift starts with leaders who are willing to enter conversations as partners, not controllers. Who ask, "How do we improve this?" and genuinely mean it. They create space for people to think, contribute, and shape what happens next.

An invitation to lead differently

The leadership approach in this book is simple:

- Invite people into conversations that help them, and you, understand work more deeply.
- Create the conditions where people can think together with clarity, courage, and care.

- Help the system stay in contact with itself so that what matters becomes visible.
- Support responsibility by cultivating shared purpose, not compliance.
- Show up in ways that signal humility, humanity, and respect.

It's a way of leading, a way of influencing without dominating, a way of moving an organisation forward by moving with it rather than against it. It is how progress is made in human, interconnected work.

This doesn't mean you stop making decisions or require consensus on everything. It doesn't mean leadership becomes passive or permissive. Authority still matters, standards still matter, and accountability still matters.

What changes is how those things are exercised, which is through relationship rather than control. Through partnership rather than enforcement, and through building "we" rather than managing "them".

The question isn't whether you have the authority to lead differently. You do. The question is whether you're willing to use that authority to create the conditions where others can lead too. Where frontline intelligence can reach decision-making. Where weak signals can travel. Where "we" becomes the way the organisation works together.

CHAPTER 12

Developing Conversational Mastery

When I first started having conversations with frontline workers about their work, I didn't really know what I was doing. I had five years of training as a psychologist and a head full of theoretical ideals. I believed in learning from normal work, in capturing people's stories, in the value of describing rather than comparing. But I didn't yet know how to ask better questions. I didn't know how to build rapport quickly. I didn't know how to guide a conversation in a way that felt natural for the person and useful for the organisation.

And I was doing all of this in a new country, in my second language, with a managing director who had committed me to a headline construction project. People were expecting something meaningful and impressive. But there was no map. I simply had to begin.

I still clearly remember one of my first site conversations. I was speaking with someone who said their job was as a "sparky". I had to ask what that was. Turns out it's an electrician. That incompetence didn't mess anything up but promoted a kinder, warmer connection with my conversation partner.

We went on to talk about the work he was doing, what was unique to this site. About halfway through he mentioned that the drawings were a mess because there had been so many revisions, so they were crowded with details. He'd brought a magnifying glass to help decipher the plans. He pulled it out of his breast pocket and showed me – a foldable lens with a padded cover.

As I walked away from that conversation, I smiled. From the stumbling and nervous opening, the conversation had become a place of trust where I was shown details of how work got done. I felt like I was sitting on a small but valuable secret. I felt grateful.

People wanted to talk about their work. After initial scepticism came warmth, curiosity, and sudden moments of powerful insight. These early conversations fuelled the sense that careful attention to this work might matter.

I began reading more widely. I became more intentional about my conversations. I started collecting questions. I experimented with different ways to open a conversation, different directions to explore, different ways to make sense of what people were telling me. I recorded my conversations and listened back to reflect on what was happening. I learned how to bring the conversation back to shared inquiry, so it became collaborative rather than extractive. And, eventually, I realised that what I was learning could help other people. I started training and coaching, and in time, this book began to form.

Conversational mastery emerges from practise with real people in real situations – noticing, adjusting, and trying again. Reading helps, but the craft requires getting out from behind your desk to talk *with* people, not *to* them. Conversational mastery grows through experience, reflection, and a willingness to keep learning, even when you think you've already "got it".

This chapter traces the developmental journey from first stumbling steps to helping others take theirs, gradually expanding capacity until you become someone who helps organisations think, feel, and learn together.

The journey of mastery

What follows isn't a linear path but an expanding spiral of capacity. Think of it as four developmental stages, each building on the previous ones while opening new territory. You don't complete one and move to the next. Rather, each stage adds new dimensions to your practice while deepening what came before.

The first stage is about waking up to yourself as an instrument and developing deliberate skill. The second expands your capacity to stay present with difficulty and emotion. The third shifts your focus from individual conversations to seeing the systems those conversations reveal. The fourth moves you from personal mastery to shaping organisational capacity – leading through conversation and multiplying your impact through others.

At every stage, you return to the fundamentals of presence, curiosity, genuine questions, and careful listening. The basics never stop mattering, they just get applied in wider and more complex contexts as your capacity grows.

Stage 1: Awareness and practising

Most people arrive believing they're already skilled conversationalists. Years of talking with crews and colleagues, asking questions, putting people at ease ... or so they think. The first developmental shift happens when you start seeing yourself as an instrument, not just a participant. Paying attention to conversation as understanding rather than mere coordination reveals habits as if from outside: how quickly you try to help, how often your questions are really statements, how rarely you sit in silence long enough for someone to say the harder thing, how much your presence shapes what other people feel able to say.

The first time I noticed my conversational habits was while listening to a recording of myself facilitating a group discussion. Bracing for the sound of my voice proved uncomfortable but expected. However, the surprise came elsewhere. Silence barely existed because I filled every pause. Another question always stood ready, another prompt to move things along. It sounded competent, engaged, professional. But as I kept listening, I sensed a pattern emerging. Each time I stepped in, I subtly steered the conversation. Without meaning to, I also signalled that it was time to move on from whatever had just been said.

In one moment, someone started sharing something that mattered to them. There was a small pause. Listening back, it was clear they weren't finished. The silence felt like a check-in, maybe even an invitation for someone else to lean in. But I jumped in with a new question about something completely different. And in doing so, I closed something that hadn't yet opened.

It was painful to listen to, but it was the beginning of becoming aware of my own conversational patterns.

At this stage, patterns will become visible to you. You'll notice interruptions, body language that leans forward for preferred answers and backward otherwise, silences filled from discomfort, the urge to soothe upset people (which is really about reducing your own discomfort), questions like "Why did you do that?", which trigger defensiveness despite genuine curiosity. The gap between intention and impact reveals itself. Interest reads as interrogation, helpfulness becomes takeover, and listening masks waiting-to-speak.

Such noticing may be uncomfortable. The point is simply to start seeing your conversational habits more clearly without harsh judgement. Treat patterns as information, not indictment.

Once patterns become visible, ignoring them proves difficult. Awareness leads naturally towards intention. You begin experimenting, trying one good question instead of a list, waiting a beat longer before speaking, staying with their example rather than steering towards your agenda, or noticing when pace, posture, or tone changes.

Each conversation becomes an experiment:

- Before the conversation, pick one thing to try.
- During it, notice whether it's happening.
- After, reflect on what you observed and what you'll adjust next time.

In June 2014, I spent two weeks in rural New South Wales, talking with coal-mining crews about what got in the way of good work. For days, I asked about breakdowns and difficulties. The stories came easily. After a while, I noticed something in myself. I was saturated. Tired. I had little capacity left to take in more accounts of what was hard or broken. One evening, I called a friend and vented. He listened, then said, "What if you tried asking about where the good comes from instead?"

The next day, I experimented. I began asking about moments when things worked unusually well, when people went beyond what was required. It was awkward at first as people weren't sure what I was after. But I stayed with it. Slowly, I learned which questions opened something and which fell flat. I learned that a clumsy question doesn't end a conversation. You can pause, adjust, and keep going. Practice is how you learn to stay in the dance.

The goal isn't perfect performance but learning steps, moves, sequences, and gradually expanding the tools that feel natural.

Experiments to try

Start with these practices and notice what happens:

- The three-second pause. After someone finishes speaking, count to three. This creates space for them to add more while giving you time to respond rather than react.
- "Tell me more." Use this phrase twice per conversation at a minimum, and make sure it's driven by genuine curiosity. What else exists here? What remains unseen?
- Ask for examples. When someone offers an opinion or generalisation, respond with, "Can you give me an example of when that happened?" Opinions are useful, but examples are where truth lives.
- Follow their thread. When someone mentions something in passing, like a frustration, a worry, or a small detail, resist the urge to move on to your agenda. Follow their thread by asking, "You mentioned that was frustrating. What made it frustrating?"
- Record yourself and listen back. Patterns that are likely to stand out are airtime ratios, frequency of redirects, and questions that opened space versus those that closed it.

- Ask for feedback: "What did you notice about me in that conversation?" Their observations are information, not judgement.
- Name your internal state during conversations; for example, "I'm feeling defensive right now," or "I'm getting impatient." Just naming it creates a tiny space between the impulse and your action.
- After important conversations, note what you tried, what happened, what you noticed about yourself and them, what you're learning, and what you'll try next. Five minutes of reflection teaches more than five hours of reading about technique.

You're developing the capacity to be able to adjust your approach mid-conversation, experiment naturally without it feeling forced, notice what works and doesn't in real time, build a repertoire of moves that feel genuinely yours, and trust the conversation more than your agenda. At some point, the practices stop feeling like techniques you're applying and start feeling like natural responses. That's when you're ready for the next stage.

Stage 2: Holding difficulty

As your intentional practice deepens, new capacity emerges, where you can stay grounded through difficult, emotional, or uncertain conversations. The ability to hold more human experience without tidying it up develops. The work becomes harder and more rewarding.

Staying present through frustration or scepticism becomes possible, and longer silences feel manageable. You start sensing when someone has more to say, despite words suggesting otherwise. You resist the urge to smooth over discomfort, knowing truth often sits there.

"What do you wish they had explained better during your site induction?" I once asked a mining truck operator who was a relative newcomer.

"How to navigate this site," he said.

He described being shown a map during training. Here is the digger. Here is the dump. Here are the intersections. Watch out for other vehicles ... But once signed off, he was left to figure out the real navigation on his own, and reality doesn't look like the map.

I felt an urge to help the story along, to solve it, to extract the workaround I assumed must be there. Instead, I stayed quiet.

After a pause, he added that calling for help on the radio felt risky. As a new employee asking for guidance on an intersection everyone else seemed to know, he feared the commentary wouldn't stop. I waited.

He looked at me, smiled slightly, and said, "So I kept waiting until another truck came along. Then I followed them."

The intelligence, vulnerability, and care in his judgement were obvious. When we slow down enough to give people space, they often show us more than we expected.

Holding difficulty isn't about fixing it, rescuing people from it, making it comfortable, having all the answers, or collapsing it into something simple. It means staying present while someone struggles, letting tension exist without rushing to resolve it, allowing emotion without managing it, creating space for contradiction, and trusting that understanding will emerge.

This requires staying with your own discomfort, noticing your body's signals, such as the tightness, heat, the urge to rescue or control. Name the feelings without acting on them. Breathe, soften your shoulders, then return attention to the other person.

When emotion arrives, resist fixing or redirecting. Stay present, keep breathing, and offer simple acknowledgement:

"This matters to you." Wait until the wave passes because sometimes being heard suffices. Steadiness provides the gift, not solutions.

You're growing the capacity to be able to stay present when someone becomes emotional without needing to fix it, where you can let difficult silences stretch without filling them, you notice your own reactions without acting on them, you hold contradictory perspectives without collapsing them, and you help people feel steady even when content is hard.

Once you can hold difficulty in the room – staying present with emotion, contradiction, and uncertainty – a new kind of seeing becomes possible. You notice that different people's experiences, while seeming contradictory, often reveal different facets of the same larger pattern. You're sensing the system.

Stage 3: Seeing systems

The most profound shift in conversational practice comes when you abandon the search for THE truth and begin collecting truths. Plural, multiple, and sometimes contradictory.

In 2016, I was working with an aircraft maintenance operation outside Adelaide. Equipment shortages dominated every conversation, but each group I spoke with described the problem completely differently. Frontline crews spoke about missing stands, shared ladders, fall-arrest gear rarely being where it was needed. Another group described equipment being taken by crews claiming what they needed before others got it. Supervisors framed it as a coordination and relationship issue, as tension between contractors and employees, and poor sharing norms. A senior leader traced it back to early mobilisation decisions, starting work before procurement and logistics were ready.

It was the same situation but wildly different accounts. Each made sense from where the person stood, and together they revealed a system slowly coming into view.

If you only hear one voice, you'll design the wrong intervention. If you try to reconcile them into a single story, you'll lose the nuance. But if you can hold all pictures simultaneously, you begin to see the system.

Two related capacities develop at this stage:

- Hearing multiple perspectives without choosing between them, collecting them like puzzle pieces.
- Seeing how pieces connect into larger patterns. Stories from different parts echo each other, and the system speaks through people's experiences.

You begin seeing patterns across contexts, structural causes beneath behaviour, and connections between organisational levels. What looked like individual failure reveals itself as rational response to systemic pressure. The invisible becomes visible – the unspoken expectations shaping behaviour, the trade-offs people make that never appear in reports, the informal systems holding formal systems together, and the gap between what the organisation says and what it rewards.

Systems are messy. They contain contradictions that can't be resolved, only managed. You develop tolerance for unsatisfying answers, competing truths, and problems without clear solutions. Your language shifts to, "Both of these are true," "This is more complicated than it first appeared," "There's no root cause, but lots of contributing factors," "We might need to hold this tension rather than resolve it." This doesn't mean paralysis. It means staying with difficulty long enough to respond wisely rather than quickly.

In the autumn of 2016, I facilitated a workshop to improve mining operations efficiency. One conversation was about prestart meetings. The frontline crews said the meetings were ineffective and confusing. After prestarts, people sometimes spent ten or fifteen minutes trying to work out what they were actually doing that day.

A supervisor had a clear explanation: "The problem is people are lazy. They don't listen. They sit there half asleep with their hard hats over their eyes. We need consequences."

The group went quiet. If we accepted that explanation too quickly, the conversation would close. So, I paused and said, "Okay, that might explain one part of the picture. What else could be going on?"

What followed was a widening. Someone pointed to the time available – eight minutes to pass on all information – while someone else noted the number of people – more than eighty – receiving individual instructions. Another mentioned the screen – only people at the front could see it. I kept asking, "What else? What else might be making this hard?"

More details surfaced. Sometimes breathalyser tests and crib arrangements happened simultaneously with the prestart. The room itself was poor for listening; it was dirty, dim, with noisy air-conditioning. Sometimes the delivery wasn't easy to follow.

By the end, we weren't "aligned" in the corporate sense. We were simply wiser. We had a more faithful picture of what was making the prestarts ineffective. And with that shared picture, better options started to suggest themselves.

You know you're developing the capacity to see systems when you naturally collect multiple perspectives before forming conclusions, you see patterns others miss, you can explain why something happens without blaming individuals, you hold contradictions without needing to resolve them immediately, and you can help people say, “I hadn’t thought of it that way.”

This stage transforms you from a skilled conversationalist into someone who can help an organisation understand itself. You’re revealing the living system those stories point to. And once you can see the system, you’re ready to begin shaping the conversations the organisation needs to learn about itself.

Stage 4: Leading and multiplying impact

Until now, capacity has developed within conversations. This final stage marks intentional use of that capacity on behalf of the system: the shift from participant to leader, from skilled practitioner to someone shaping an organisation’s conversational life and growing that capacity in others.

In 2023, a utilities company asked me to help roll out their “Golden Rules”. On paper, the task was straightforward – build understanding, reduce resistance, and create internal champions. But they were already sensing that another round of presentations wouldn’t go deep enough.

What struck me was the relative coherence of the ten Golden Rules, and what I assumed must be the diverse mess of people’s experience underneath. That told me the organisation didn’t need better messaging. It needed a different conversation.

So, instead of running a traditional engagement session, we convened small groups of eight to ten people from across roles. The invitation was simple: let’s talk about what these rules really mean in your work.

What began as a discussion about definitions quickly shifted. A rigger pointed out that one rule looked simple on a poster but relied on constant judgement in the field. A technician described how the same rule played out very differently in remote locations compared to the workshop. An office-based participant admitted they didn't really understand what "working at height" meant beyond the wording.

As these perspectives met, the rules stopped being abstract statements and became shared reference points. Understanding emerged from people thinking together, testing assumptions, filling in each other's blind spots.

At the end, I asked everyone to choose the Golden Rule that mattered most to them and explain why. One person wrote, *Because today I finally understand what this rule is trying to achieve, and I agree with it.*

In under an hour, the rules had shifted from corporate broadcast to collective meaning.

Recognising when conversation is needed

Leadership at this stage begins with noticing. You pay attention to when the official story is drifting from lived reality, when patterns need names, when pressure is reshaping work quietly but significantly, when a tension needs space, when understanding isn't enough and the conversation needs to shift from "what" to "now what", or after a significant event when the organisation needs to make sense of it together before moving on. You don't wait to be asked. You recognise the need and create the space.

Convening well requires design thinking. Who belongs in the room? The answer is those with lived experience of the issue, those with authority to act, those holding perspectives that need to meet, and those who'll be affected by the outcomes. The smallest group that can see the whole picture.

What question focuses the conversation? This isn't a topic but a question that invites real thinking, such as, "What's making good work hard right now?" or "What are we not talking about that we need to talk about?"

Frame the invitation so it signals that this will be different from usual meetings, that your experience matters here. We're here to think together.

Design the opening so that people can shift from their previous meeting into this space. Host the middle by shaping conditions, such as pace, voice balance, and depth. Close in a way that names what has formed, what stays unresolved, and what happens next.

When designing the Golden Rules conversations, I convened small groups with deliberately mixed roles, knowing diversity of experience would surface richer questions. Rather than discussing rules abstractly, I designed an activity requiring interaction. Each Golden Rule was printed on a card, and groups placed them along different continuums. The framing lowered the risk of being wrong and invited critique. People didn't need polished opinions, they needed to talk to each other. As people debated placement, stories surfaced naturally. Understanding emerged through exchange, not explanation.

Growing capacity in others

Real organisational change requires conversation to spread beyond you. Individual mastery, no matter how developed, has limits. The work becomes making yourself redundant.

At the start of a leadership program in 2024, most of the participants rated themselves as highly confident in having safety conversations. Layla was no exception. An experienced project manager, she was decisive and direct. If she saw a non-conformance, she addressed it immediately. Things got fixed.

Early on, I asked her a question that unsettled her: "What happens after you walk around the corner?" How confident was she that the change would hold when she wasn't there? That question stayed with her.

Over the following months, I worked with Layla through an extended coaching program. We focused on small experiments. She began by choosing five questions she wanted to try in real conversations. They were simple, curious questions. When she came back, she was surprised how people started talking more openly; they offered context she hadn't heard before.

Next, she noticed she was still doing most of the talking. Together, we explored what might happen if she held silence just a little longer. That was uncomfortable for her at first, but gradually, the pauses started to fill themselves. As her confidence grew, she stopped arriving with answers and started bringing back insights. Stories of how teams were adapting work and the ideas that came from others, not from her.

Each month, we set one small stretch. Nothing dramatic, but just enough to keep her learning at the edge of her comfort. Eventually, the conversations no longer depended on her authority. They worked because people trusted the space she'd created.

Growing conversational capacity in others demands different skills than personal practice. Look for people who already listen well but don't know they have skill, are frustrated with surface conversations, have natural curiosity about how work really happens, hold informal influence, or show up with presence and care.

Help them see their patterns. For example, "I noticed you jumped in to fix that. What were you feeling?" Create practice opportunities through co-facilitating, leading small conversations while you observe, debriefing afterwards. Have conversations about conversations: "What made that question work well?" "When did you lose the thread?"

Let them find their own style. Some people are naturally slow and spacious, while others are energetic and probing. Help them find what's authentic for them, not what works for you.

Creating the conditions

Individual skill matters but isn't sufficient alone. Organisational conditions must keep conversation alive. It's important to create regular spaces for genuine dialogue, not reporting meetings, such as through weekly learning conversations, monthly story-sharing sessions, quarterly sensemaking forums, or leadership huddles for honest reflection.

Help stories travel by retelling good stories in different contexts, asking, "What are you hearing from the field?" in meetings, creating simple ways for stories to be shared, and helping people see when their local story has wider relevance.

Build infrastructure by having time in schedules for reflection, giving permission to raise difficult topics, providing a response when people speak (something changes as a result), and recognition for those who host good conversations.

Protect conversational space from performance pressure. Advocate for qualitative indicators over metrics. Help leaders understand how measurement kills what it tracks. Share impact stories without reducing them to numbers.

Eventually, if the work succeeds, conversation shifts from something you do to something the organisation does. Signals emerge, like conversations happening without you, stories travelling independently, leaders asking different questions, issues surfacing earlier, and "We should talk about this" replacing workarounds.

Support without controlling, trust what's emerging, and let people find their own way. Celebrate what's working and stay available without being central.

Sometimes I hear a story being retold and realise, halfway through, that I was part of its beginning. The first time this happened, I felt an impulse to correct it, to clarify what really happened. But then I thought, *The story is travelling without me. People are using it to make sense of their own situations. It no longer belongs to me. It belongs to the organisation.* So, I didn't polish it or protect it. I let it become what people needed. I was pleased that the work was spreading.

A paradox often emerges where growing skill at developing others' conversational capacity makes you less necessary. But this is the intended outcome. The goal isn't building dependency on your expertise but organisational capability to stay in conversation with itself, noticing its own drift, hearing its own signals, and thinking together about what matters. Distributed across many people, this capacity makes organisations more intelligent, adaptive, and humane.

You're developing the capacity of leading and multiplying impact when you recognise when conversation is needed before being asked, you can convene the right people around the right question, you help groups think better together, you hear people say, "This was different from our usual meetings," you see insight emerge that no one person brought, you feel comfortable holding space without controlling outcomes, you get asked to facilitate important conversations, you notice conversations happening without you, and you watch capacity growing in people you've coached.

Foundational practices

Across all stages, certain practices remain constant:

- Steadiness means staying present when conversations heat up or tilt sideways.
- Ethical responsibility is holding people's stories with care, never using them against those who offered them.
- Micro-skills include the pause, the "tell me more", the well-timed silence.
- Repair is circling back when you rush past something, naming missteps, showing that the conversation matters more than your performance.

At the heart of these practices sit the three qualities from Chapter 3: curiosity that stays open, compassion that holds difficulty, and courage that remains present. These aren't techniques to master sequentially but foundations you return to again and again, even as your capacity expands.

Where are you now?

Take a moment to locate yourself. Where is your growing edge? What's one practice that would help you move forward? Who could support you?

This work develops through practise, reflection, and willingness to keep learning. Each conversation is an opportunity. Each mistake is information. Your organisation needs you to keep developing.

After fifteen-plus years of doing this type of work, I still catch myself rushing to fix, avoiding discomfort, steering towards preferred answers. The difference is noticing sooner, adjusting more easily, and trusting the process more deeply.

Mastery means staying willing to engage with questions and challenges, not controlling conversation but trusting it enough to follow where it leads.

This craft is simple in principle, but demanding in practice, and it's essential to the work of helping organisations become more honest and more intelligent. The work continues with your next conversation.

Afterword

I'm writing this on a Saturday morning in Brisbane. My son Charlie, who's seven, just asked me what I'm working on.

"A book to help people at work talk to each other," I said.

"Talk about what?"

"About how work is going, what's working well, what's difficult. And what's dangerous."

He thought about this for a moment. "Do they listen to each other?"

I smiled. "That's the whole point."

He nodded, seemingly satisfied, and went back to building his Formula 1 Lego car.

Out of the mouths of seven year olds.

Do they listen to each other?

That's what this entire book comes down to. Not techniques or frameworks or conversation types. Not the perfect question or the right phrase at the right moment. Just, do they listen to each other?

And underneath that, do they *want* to listen to each other?

Because if they don't, if the person asking the question is really just waiting to correct, or verify compliance, or move on to the next item on their checklist, then nothing in this book will help. No framework, no matter how elegant, can substitute for genuine care about another person's experience.

But if they do want to listen, if there's real curiosity about how work happens, real compassion for what people navigate, real courage to hear things that might be uncomfortable, then the techniques almost don't matter. The conversation will find its way.

I've spent fifteen years learning this work, and I'm still learning it. Just last week I caught myself rushing through a conversation because I "knew" where it was going. I had to stop myself, apologise, and ask the person to start again. They did, and what they said the second time was completely different from what I'd assumed they were going to say.

I still fill silences when I should let them breathe. I still offer solutions when I should stay with understanding. I still reach for control when I should trust the process (just ask my wife).

The difference now is that I notice it sooner. I can adjust mid-conversation. I trust that recovering from a misstep is part of the practice, not evidence of failure.

And I've learned to be gentler with myself about this. Conversation is not a skill you master and then possess. It's a practice you return to, again and again, with as much presence as you can bring in this moment, with this person, about this work.

If you've read this far, you might be feeling one of two things.

You might be feeling inspired, ready to have different conversations, to show up differently, to create space where truth can be spoken. If that's you, I'm grateful. Go have that conversation. Start with curiosity, stay with compassion, and find your courage. See what happens.

Or you might be feeling overwhelmed, aware of all the ways your current conversations fall short, all the habits you've suddenly noticed, all the work ahead. If that's you, I want to say, start small. One conversation, one quality, one choice to ask, "How do we improve this?" instead of "How do I get you to do this?"

You just have to show up a little more honestly in your next conversation.

That's enough. That's where it starts.

I think about the people whose stories appear in these pages.

The tower painters at Transpower who spent years being told to try harder, until someone finally asked them what they needed.

The technician who spent five days looking for a thermometer, whose small truth helped an entire organisation see itself differently.

The mining truck operator who learned by following others because asking for help felt too risky.

Sarah, the truck driver with systems thinking that no job description captures.

The stores person who'd stopped speaking up because nothing ever changed.

The kitchen crew who learned that asking for help was professional, not weak.

None of them were waiting for perfect conversations. They were waiting for genuine ones. For someone to show up with real curiosity, real compassion, and real courage. For someone to see them as partners in making work work better, not as problems to manage.

When that happened, when the conversation was finally real, change began. Not because of the techniques being used, but because of the relationship being built.

There's a question that sits underneath everything in this book. It's not stated explicitly anywhere, but it runs through every chapter, every story, every framework.

The question is: What kind of organisation do you want to be?

Do you want to be one that maintains the us/them divide, where leadership decides and workers comply, where distance is managed through control, where weak signals die in the gap between roles?

Or do you want to be one that builds "we", where people think together across difference, where truth can travel, and where understanding is shared before solutions are imposed?

This is not a question about safety programs or culture initiatives. It's about relationship, how you relate to the people doing the work, and whether you see them as instruments to manage or partners to work with.

Every conversation is an answer to that question.

- When you arrive on site with a checklist, you're answering it one way. When you arrive with genuine curiosity, you're answering it another.
- When you respond to a concern with defensiveness, you're answering it one way. When you respond with "Tell me more", you're answering it another.
- When you impose a solution without understanding the problem, you're answering it one way. When you ask, "How do we make this work?" you're answering it another.

The question is being answered every day, in hundreds of small interactions. The real work is making those answers intentional.

I started this book by saying that conversation is the "talking cure" for organisations. That just as therapy creates space for what has been avoided to finally be named and integrated, conversation allows organisations to acknowledge what they've been unable to see.

I still believe that. But I've also come to see that conversation is more than cure. It's also prevention, maintenance, and growth:

- Prevention: When people can speak honestly about pressures and trade-offs before they become incidents.
- Maintenance: When the organisation stays in regular contact with itself, noticing drift before it becomes fracture.
- Growth: When understanding expands through dialogue, when intelligence is distributed rather than concentrated, when "we" becomes stronger than "us and them".

Organisations that practise conversation don't just avoid harm more effectively. They learn faster, adapt better, and treat people more humanely. This isn't because they've eliminated hierarchy or structure or accountability, but because they've learned to exercise those things through relationship rather than control.

That's what becomes possible when conversation moves from performance to practice. When it stops being something you do to people and becomes something you do with them.

I don't know where you'll take this work. Maybe you're a safety professional who'll use these ideas to shift how you engage with frontline crews. Maybe you're a supervisor who'll start asking different questions in prestart meetings. Maybe you're a senior leader who'll create space for the conversations your organisation has been avoiding. Maybe you're someone who just wants to listen better, to stay more present, to create more humanity in how you show up at work.

Wherever you are, whatever your role, the work is the same – to help truth travel. Close the distance between people, and build "we" where there has been separation.

Start with your next conversation. Not the perfect conversation, just the next one:

- Show up with curiosity about how work really happens.
- Stay with compassion for what people navigate.
- Find the courage to hear what's uncomfortable.
- Ask, "How do we improve this?" instead of "How do I get you to do this?"

Then see what happens.

Charlie just came back, with the Lego car complete.

"Want to see?" he asked.

"Show me how you built it," I said. "What was the most difficult part?"

He lit up. For the next ten minutes, he walked me through his process, what was difficult, mistakes he made, where he got confused by the instructions, how he backtracked and corrected.

I didn't offer suggestions for improvement. I just listened, asked questions when I didn't understand, and let him teach me about his work.

When he finished, he looked satisfied, not because I'd praised him, but because we'd shared a nice moment, I think.

It's not that different with adults, really.

People want their work to be seen. They want their intelligence to be recognised. They want to contribute to making things better, and they want to be part of "we".

The conversation that makes that possible doesn't require perfection. It just requires presence. And it starts with the simple question my seven-year-old asked, "Do they listen to each other?"

May your answer be yes.

Brisbane, Australia
February, 2026

PS. If you'd like a practical summary of the conversation types in this book, I've put together a free companion guide at safetyconversations.com.

– D

Acknowledgements

This book emerged from fifteen years of conversations with people doing difficult work under real conditions. I am grateful to everyone who trusted me with their stories, frustrations, and insights. To the tradies, safety professionals, supervisors, and managers in workshops over the years who tested these ideas and told me what worked, this book is better because you were honest about what didn't. Your willingness to speak honestly about how work actually happens and what matters to you gave this book its foundation.

I'm forever grateful to David Bond, a seriously great human being. He trusted me and offered opportunities for me to stretch my wings in talking to people. His belief in me shaped my practice more than any formal method ever could. Without David, this book would not exist.

Ron Gantt has been a collaborator and avid supporter. Generous with his time, thoughtful in his challenge, steady in moments of doubt. His own story about the construction site shutdown (Chapter 9) shows the kind of leader he is. Everyone should have someone like Ron in their corner.

Rob Cousins read more versions of this manuscript than anyone. His honest, practical, and sometimes confronting feedback helped turn a loose collection of reflections into ideas that could stand on their own. If this book makes sense to practitioners, it's because Rob insisted it must.

Tony Hetherington was the first person I trusted with early draft chapters. An experienced high-hazard safety regulator, he brought a depth of care and curiosity to his reading, and validation that the book was relevant and needed. His encouragement mattered more than he probably realised.

Jop Havinga has been a thinking partner throughout this journey. Many of the ideas in these pages emerged through long conversations over dinner and drinks in Brisbane. Thoughtful, pragmatic, and relentlessly curious, Jop helped me make sense of the way work happens and can be understood. I look forward to continuing those conversations.

Shirlene Vautier offered encouragement and feedback throughout the writing process, always meeting the work with enthusiasm and generosity. Her belief in what this book could become kept me writing when the path forward felt unclear.

Helen Rawlinson encouraged me to share what I had learned more widely. She trusted me to carry and tell some of the stories that appear in these pages, and her confidence in the work helped me believe it was worth finishing.

I also want to acknowledge Andy Brogan of Easier Inc. I have never met Andy, nor have we ever spoken, but his thinking has nonetheless shaped my work in quiet and enduring ways. Through his writing and generous sharing online, Andy has consistently articulated a view of people and performance that resists simplification and refuses blame. His insistence on seeing work as it is lived, on respecting human effort, and on questioning easy explanations has influenced how I notice organisations, how I listen to people, and how I think about improvement. This book carries traces of that influence, particularly the relational patterns that show up as "us and them" versus "we". His generous reflections helped me notice language and dynamics I now see everywhere in safety, leadership, and change work. For that intellectual generosity, I am grateful.

Many clients, colleagues, and contacts over the years have shaped what this book has become: Ruth Denyer, Rene van der Merwe, Mark Collins, Phil Parkes, Anna Keen, Drew Rae, Soraya Alsultan, Paulo Gomes, Roel van Winsen, Andy Shone, Kadie Brown, Becky Picton, Adam Johns, Zinta Satins, Richmond Johnston, Katie Muldrew, John Green among many others. Each brought challenge, development, and meaning to my work. I am grateful for what I learned from you.

To the organisations that opened their doors and allowed me to learn from their people: Squadron Energy, Landcare Research, Digital Realty and the many mining, construction, aviation, and utilities operations I've worked with, thank you for trusting me with access to your reality.

Finally, Marion Revelli. Your support, patience, and willingness to give me the space this work required made more difference than you know. You read drafts, listened to ideas that weren't yet clear, and believed in this book even when I wasn't sure it would come together. Thank you for standing alongside me as it took shape.

The stories in this book belong to the people who lived them. Any wisdom here is theirs. The mistakes are mine alone.

About the author

Daniel Hummerdal works at the intersection of safety, organisational development, and psychology, helping organisations translate frontline experience into systemic learning. He supports mining, construction, aviation, and utilities operations to build conversational capacity, which is the ability to stay in honest contact with how work unfolds.

Originally trained as a commercial pilot in Sweden, Daniel's path into this field began through accident investigation. Drawn to the human dimensions of safety, he later re-trained to graduate as a psychologist, seeking to understand not only what goes wrong, but how human capability can be engaged to make work safer and better.

Over the past fifteen years, Daniel has developed a practice grounded in conversation rather than control. His focus is on creating conditions where frontline experience can reach leadership, weak signals can travel, and people can think together about how work is really done. He is less interested in providing answers than in helping organisations ask better questions of themselves.

Daniel lives in Brisbane, Australia, with his wife, Marion, and their two sons, Charlie and Elliot. *An Introduction to Safety Conversations* is his first book.

Sources and further reading

Chapter 1

Andrew, A. (2018). *Ensuring contractors are successful–so you can be too*. Business Leaders' Health & Safety Forum/Safetree.

Chapter 2

Hollnagel, E. (2018). *Safety-II in practice: Developing the resilience potentials*. Routledge.

Hopkins, A. (2011). *Management walk-arounds: Lessons from the Gulf of Mexico oil well blowout* (Working Paper No. 79). National Research Centre for OHS Regulation, Australian National University.

Chapter 3

Edmondson, A. C. (2018). *The fearless organization: Creating psychological safety in the workplace for learning, innovation, and growth*. John Wiley & Sons.

Schein, E. H. (2013). *Humble inquiry: The gentle art of asking instead of telling*. Berrett-Koehler Publishers.

Chapter 6

Cooperrider, D. L., & Whitney, D. (2005). *Appreciative inquiry: A positive revolution in change*. Berrett-Koehler Publishers.

Pascale, R., Sternin, J., & Sternin, M. (2010). *The power of positive deviance: How unlikely innovators solve the world's toughest problems*. Harvard Business Press.

Chapter 7

Mohanty, R. P., & Deshmukh, S. G. (1999). "Managing the quality circle process: A new investigation of Toyota's QC practices." *Production Planning & Control*, 10(4), 357–368.

Chapter 8

Sinek, S. (2009). *Start with why: How great leaders inspire everyone to take action*. Portfolio.

Stepczak, P. (2025). [LinkedIn post on co-design and engagement]. Retrieved from LinkedIn, 7 February 2026.

Chapter 9

Brown, B. (2018). *Dare to lead: Brave work, tough conversations, whole hearts*. Random House.

Zehr, H. (2015). *The little book of restorative justice: Revised and updated*. Good Books.

Chapter 10

Bushe, G. R., & Marshak, R. J. (Eds.). (2015). *Dialogic organization development: The theory and practice of transformational change*. Berrett-Koehler Publishers.

Callahan, S. (2016). *Putting stories to work: Mastering business storytelling*. Pepperberg Press.

Chapter 11

Freud, S., & Breuer, J. (1955). *Studies on hysteria* (J. Strachey, Trans.). Basic Books. (Original work published 1895)

Index

A

B

C

D

E

M

N

O

P

R

S

T

W

www.ingramcontent.com/pod-product-compliance
Ingram Content Group UK Ltd.
Pitfield, Milton Keynes, MK11 3LW, UK
UKHW021036270726
13967UKWH00013B/2809